Praise for *Reinventing Social Change*

"This is truly a book for our moment. Nell Edgington gives concrete, actionable advice for how social change leaders can move from a scarcity mindset to one of abundance, and in the process heal our broken world. Her mantra, "change yourself, change the system, change the world" has never felt more urgent or more necessary."

KATHY REICH, director, BUILD (Building Institutions and Networks) at the Ford Foundation

"If you're working to make social change, this book will help you break free of the dogmas that so often hold nonprofit leaders and other changemakers back. In crisp and hard-hitting prose, Nell Edgington offers a roadmap for how leaders can empower themselves and those around them, articulate desired outcomes and align resources to achieve them, and fundraise to cover the real costs of what it takes to make change. Both inspirational and practical, *Reinventing Social Change* helps leaders get the best out of themselves, their staff, board, volunteers, and broader network—in service of changing the world at a time of unparalleled challenge. Edgington draws on her decades of experience working with— and deep respect for—social change leaders to call on all of us to be our very best."

PHIL BUCHANAN, president, Center for Effective Philanthropy, and author of *Giving Done Right: Effective Philanthropy and Making Every Dollar Count*

D0188321

"In *Reinventing Social Change*, Nell Edgington helps us see how nonprofit and philanthropic leaders can become more powerful, well-resourced, and energized agents of social change. Full of tactical frameworks and compelling case studies, this book helps social change leaders understand how to overcome what may be holding them back, and attract and mobilize the money and people they need to achieve their goals. Informed by her almost twenty-five years of experience consulting to nonprofits and philanthropy, this book is sure to be an important playbook for social change leaders in the post-pandemic world."

KATHLEEN P. ENRIGHT, president and CEO, Council on Foundations

"Nell Edgington's new book provides a roadmap for nonprofit leaders who need to navigate in a post-pandemic world with limited resources to create positive change. It is a must-read for nonprofit leaders to help them attract more people and resources to their work."

BETH KANTER, nonprofit innovator, and author of *The Happy, Healthy Nonprofit*

"Equal parts love letter and forceful call to action, *Reinventing Social Change* challenges social change leaders to step into our power and avoid the traps that hold us back as leaders. Written from a deep well of insights about the nonprofit CEO experience, and the social sector as a whole, it is a scathing indictment of 'what has been' and an inspiring and practical guide for achieving 'what could be.'"

ANNE WALLESTAD, president and CEO, BoardSource

Reinventing Social Change

EMBRACE ABUNDANCE TO CREATE A HEALTHIER AND MORE EQUITABLE WORLD

*Re*inventing Social Change

Nell Edgington

 PAGE
TWO
BOOKS

Cataloguing in publication information is
available from Library and Archives Canada.
ISBN 978-1-77458-031-8 (paperback)
ISBN 978-1-77458-032-5 (ebook)

Page Two
www.pagetwo.com

Edited by Amanda Lewis
Copyedited by Kendra Ward
Cover design by Taysia Louie
Interior design by Setareh Ashrafologhalai

www.socialvelocity.net

Contents

Introduction: Embrace Abundant Social Change

"If you were meant to cure cancer or write a symphony or crack cold fusion and you don't do it, you not only hurt yourself, even destroy yourself. You hurt your children. You hurt me. You hurt the planet. You shame the angels who watch over you and you spite the Almighty, who created you and only you with your unique gifts, for the sole purpose of nudging the human race one millimeter farther along its path back to God."

STEVEN PRESSFIELD

AVE YOU EVER watched someone do something so beautifully, so effortlessly, so joyfully that you felt you were witnessing the work of an angel?

You may have been watching a famous singer perform, a fishmonger expertly remove the bones from a salmon, a teacher spark a new interest in a child, or a speaker move you to tears. You know the feeling. The room suddenly goes perfectly quiet. You become completely captivated by this person unfolding their gifts. It is as if God—the angels, the Universe, whatever you believe in—is suddenly before you. And in that moment you know that this person is doing exactly what she is meant to be doing; she is in the "zone," she is all in.

What if, for some reason, she were unable to deliver her obvious gifts to the world? What if she, or some other force, got in her way? What would her life be like if she had to stifle her obvious talent?

And what would the loss be for our world if she weren't able to do what she was put here to do? How incalculably sad would that be for all of us?

The truth is that this very thing happens in the social change sector much too often, and I've witnessed it far too many times. A leader—who was trying to apply her elegant solution to the growing problem of "fake news"—worn down, isolated, near tears. A nonprofit leader—who developed a supportive space for journalists to thrive—questioning whether his organization is worthy of greater donor investments. A foundation program officer—with a vision for putting the many millions of dollars under his purview to much bolder use—defeated by "we can't do that" rebuttals at every turn. A social changemaker—who discovered a way to get young people to dramatically increase their volunteer service—incessantly roadblocked by her fearful board of directors. A nonprofit leader—with a proven model for providing education to working adults—thwarted by demanding and distracting funders until she finally disbanded her organization in frustration. A social business leader—with an amazing technology solution that increases public engagement in the political process—subjected to needless hurdles placed in her way by "supportive" funders.

And perhaps you, too, have lain awake at night, terrified that you aren't going to make payroll; that a critical board member will resign; that your funders will become disinterested; that a new government policy will stop your organization in its tracks; that the endless, tireless, thankless hamster wheel you have been on for years will never, ever stop.

All these social change leaders (including you!) offer an essential solution to a critical problem facing our communities—but something is stifling the enormous gifts they have to offer the world.

At one point, all these social change leaders truly believed in their vision of a healthier, more just, more equitable world.

They believed that their initiative or service or organization would solve a key social issue. But now they are stuck in a scarcity mindset. This scarcity might look like not enough money, board support, staff, or access to decision-makers. But primarily, it is a lack of belief—in themselves, their vision, and their ability to overcome the naysayers and the hurdles in their way.

What a tragedy. For these social changemakers, to be sure. But what a tragedy for our world. What if it were possible to overcome this tragedy?

What if instead of being exhausted, worn out, ground down, disillusioned, and depressed, you were energized and inspired by your important work? What if you found joy—yes, true, unbridled joy—in your social change work every single day? What if you jumped out of bed each morning, excited to start work? What if you were surrounded by endless numbers of people who wanted to, and could, move your work forward? What if money flowed easily and endlessly to you and your organization? What if the social change you envisioned so long ago came to fruition easily and joyfully?

What if the work of social change was abundant?

It can be. You can be an abundant social change leader, creating true solutions to the social problems we face. I promise you.

But first, let me step back and define what I mean by "social change leader." A social change leader is anyone who has the ability to direct people and/or money toward creating a more equitable, healthy world—no matter how big or small their part of the world is.

What if instead of being exhausted, worn out, ground down, disillusioned, and depressed, you were energized and inspired by your important work?

When I refer to a "social change leader" I include:

- the executive director, CEO, or board member of a nonprofit that works to address larger systemic problems or inequities;

- the head of a movement, collaborative, or network charged with creating a solution to a social issue;

- the CEO, board member, or program officer of a private, public, or community foundation aimed at creating change to address a social problem;

- an individual philanthropist committed to attacking underlying problems facing society;

- the decision-maker at a government agency focused on solving social problems;

- the head of a business that exists to create financial *and* social value;

- a corporate leader who allocates philanthropic or social responsibility dollars toward social change efforts.

Because the largest group of people focused on directly creating social change is nonprofit leaders, and they have a particular set of challenges, such as fundraising, I often refer specifically to "nonprofit leaders." But the approaches contained in this book are aimed at empowering anyone leading people and directing money toward social change initiatives.

The Overwhelm We Share

From limited dollars to easily distracted board members, finicky funders, crushing norms, and unfair regulations, the challenges standing in your way are scary. I get it. I've been there. Because I have a vision for a better world, too, and I have seen that vision impeded by massive and overwhelming hurdles.

I joined the social change sector in the late 1990s, right after college. I was attracted to the belief inherent in the sector that a better world is possible. I spent my early career working in various nonprofit organizations throughout America—from a small, startup literacy organization in Portland, Oregon, to the large, sophisticated Public Broadcasting System (PBS) headquarters in Washington, D.C., to a regional food bank in Austin, Texas. Along the way, I earned an MBA because I believed that the knowledge and tools gleaned from for-profit models could potentially be adapted to the social change sector. While all the entities I worked for had critical social change missions and some committed, passionate staff and board members, they all struggled in various ways to truly grow their reach and impact.

I started Social Velocity in 2008 because I wanted to help leaders overcome the constant scarcity (of money, committed people, influence, power) that kept them from achieving the social change they sought. I combined my years of experience in the nonprofit sector and my business degree to develop guidance, frameworks, and tools for helping leaders achieve their visions. I went along happily for eight years working with amazing leaders and feeling as if we were making a collective difference.

But then the 2016 U.S. election happened. Overnight the world became, for me and so many others, such a bleak place. America—the country I was born and raised to believe was a force for healing, democracy, philanthropy, and general good in the world—had suddenly elected a president who had built a campaign around xenophobia, fear, and hatred. The disconnect was crushing to me, as I know it was for many in America and the world.

In that moment I felt I was witnessing my country turn its back on a progression toward greater equity, connection, and healing among all of its inhabitants. In a single night, I no longer believed that we would eventually reach a place where we took great care of all the earth's inhabitants and the earth itself. And, if I no longer believed that type of change was possible, I no longer understood my purpose in the world. I was suddenly lost. And because I intuitively knew that when you yourself are lost you have little hope of guiding others, I decided to take a break for a while.

At the end of 2017 I took a four-month sabbatical (still working with my clients, but no longer writing my blog or public speaking), during which I immersed myself in anything and everything that spoke to my soul. I began reading books by people like Brené Brown, Eckhart Tolle, Martha Beck, and Thích Nhất Hạnh, among others. I started meditating daily (which, believe me, was a huge departure for this die-hard, type A personality who has trouble sitting still during a ten-minute car ride). I gave up my normal mode of always going, going, going and doing, doing, doing and instead got very still. Because I had truly reached the end of my rope, I was open to anything my intuition thought might help.

Through those months of reading, meditating, and thinking, a different view of the world emerged. Perhaps 2016 was a wake-up call to all of us social changemakers to recognize and call "bullshit" on those hurdles standing in our way. Maybe the election of Donald Trump and its devastating fallout was an opportunity to explore whether the answer to overcoming those hurdles might originate inside us, in our way of thinking.

I started working with a business coach (yes, coaches need coaches!), who helped me understand that the journey I traveled—from overwhelm to this new, empowered thinking—might be part of my purpose. Perhaps in finding my own way of overcoming hurdles—both external and internal—I unknowingly stumbled on a formula that could help others. I began to map out a path that social changemakers could follow to overcome the obstacles—in both their mindset and their tactics—standing in the way of the solutions they offer the world.

The Great Reset

Then 2020 arrived and, along with it, the COVID-19 pandemic and the laying bare of so many broken systems. From racial inequality to inadequate and inequitable health care and education systems, from a dysfunctional political system to growing wealth inequality (and the extractive financial systems that perpetuate it) to a growing global climate crisis—we have come face to face with the need to completely remake our broken systems. That year ushered in a Great Reset—an opportunity to fully face and then remake all that ails us in this world.

However, the very system we have in place to address social problems—the social change sector—is itself broken. The way the nonprofit and philanthropic sector currently operates is dysfunctional. Instead of supporting, fully investing in, and advocating for these gifted social change leaders, we put unfair and defeating rules, expectations, and norms in their path. Burned-out, worn-down, or struggling social changemakers simply are not going to create the healthier, more equitable world we know we need.

You and other social change leaders—the very people working tirelessly to bring about the healing that our world so desperately needs—are being thwarted at every turn. You are growing discouraged, disheartened, and exhausted. At the same time, there is a growing need and urgency for the solutions you offer our world. The pandemic and the many broken systems it has uncovered have increased the imperative for creating stronger, more equitable, more effective systems.

This Great Reset is an opportunity to not only fix the broken health care, education, financial, and other systems to make them equitable, healthy, and strong, but also to fix the fractured system through which that very social change is accomplished.

And that's where social change leaders, like you, come in. We desperately need social changemakers who are energized, emboldened, well resourced, and fully able to marshal people, organizations, and dollars toward a better world. You have been training for this moment for years, for decades, maybe for your whole life. Maybe you felt as though you were yelling into the wind, desperately trying to focus the attention of the masses on the growing list of social problems. And you have done this while laboring under a set of unfair, burdensome norms, rules, and restrictions that have kept you from accessing the abundance of money, people, attention, and political will that your social change visions require.

This book offers you a roadmap to overcome the unfair and unhelpful system in which you have operated for years. I'll show you how to tap into your own power and attract the abundance of money and people that will allow you to achieve the social change we so desperately need.

Because I see you. I see you hanging up after a call with a discouraging funder and putting your head in your hands. I see you reliving a conversation you had with an exasperating board member as you make your morning coffee. I see you reading the news about a new regulation that will further impede your work. I see you worrying that the demand for your organization's services is growing while funding for them is not.

I know the feeling: the weight of the world feels like it rests solely on your shoulders. But it doesn't have to be like this. The work you were put here to do needs to be easier for you—we all *need* it to be easier for you. If we truly want a more just, equitable, inclusive, and engaged society, our social change leaders on the frontlines—launching and running social change organizations and movements—must be equipped with an unlimited supply of confidence, people, money, and influence.

Your future deserves to be abundant.

The Solution Is Abundant Social Change

Abundant social change is a model that helps you deliver your gifts without feeling frustrated, burned-out, or ready to give up. And if you can achieve the social change you seek, we as a community, a society, a planet will be so much better for it.

Abundant social change shows you how to bring forth the social change you seek in a joyful, inspiring, and sustainable way. It allows you to provide solutions in smart, strategic, and lasting ways. Abundant social change means:

- recognizing and refusing to play by the outworn, constricting norms and rules that pervade the social change sector;

- tapping into your inner power;

- eschewing the tired scarcity approach of the sector and instead embracing an abundance mindset;

- fully embracing money as an effective tool to achieve your social change mission; and

- strategically mobilizing your team (both inside and outside your organization) toward your shared goals.

The first step is understanding the punishing, and (let's be honest) outdated rules and norms under which you and your social change peers have been told to operate. Our society has long told social change leaders that they are not as good, as valuable, as worthy of investment as their for-profit counterparts. And the dismal part is that many social changemakers have internalized these messages. You believe (consciously or unconsciously) that you are not competent, worthy, or valuable enough. The good news is that in fully recognizing that the system, not you, is broken, you can break free of its punishing restrictions.

Once free of these limits, you can start to recognize that your true power comes from within. By finding your center, trusting your gut, seeking joy, recognizing your value and the value of your social change work, asking for help, and cultivating compassion, you can emerge a powerhouse ready to truly lead social change.

Once you've reclaimed your own power, you can then rise from the omnipresent scarcity view and embrace the abundance that is trying to reach you and your social change vision. Believe me, money, supporters, resources—everything you need to achieve your mission—want to reach you. But you first need to believe, truly believe, that abundance is out there for you—and that you deserve it.

When you fully embrace an abundance mindset, money will become your greatest ally. By understanding how money flows in and out of your organization, and structuring it to do so more effectively, you will attract as much money as you need to sustainably achieve the social change you seek.

But it's not just about money. You also want to connect to the many more people who are poised to help you achieve your social change vision. A massive team of people both inside and outside your organization have the connections, influence, ideas, and drive to help you; they simply await your direction. Mobilizing this amazing team for good is up to you.

Once you have fully embraced the path of abundant social change, so much more is possible. You can not only realize your organization's specific social change vision but also help create a more effective social change sector and, ultimately, a healthier, more just and equitable world.

There is tremendous opportunity along the path of abundant social change. You will see your life's work, your passion and ambition come to fruition. You will move from being constantly exhausted and hitting your head against the wall to witnessing a sea change: a growing number of people engaging in, investing in, advocating for, and helping to create the change you seek.

And much more importantly, your empowered, networked, abundant work will serve as an example to the larger social change sector and to the world. You will demonstrate that we can solve the many problems we face without sacrificing our health, our sanity, our gifts, or our dreams in the process.

Doesn't that sound like an opportunity worth pursuing?

It is! So, let's get to work.

Recognize The System (Not You) Is Broken

"Hope is not blind optimism. It's not ignoring the enormity of the task ahead or the roadblocks that stand in our path. It's not sitting on the sidelines or shirking from a fight. Hope is that thing inside us that insists, despite all evidence to the contrary, that something better awaits us if we have the courage to reach for it, and to work for it, and to fight for it. Hope is the belief that destiny will not be written for us, but by us, by the men and women who are not content to settle for the world as it is, who have the courage to remake the world as it should be."

BARACK OBAMA

L ET'S START WITH the brutal truth. The way we do social change is horribly broken. Knowingly or not, we have built a dysfunctional structure of restrictive norms, demoralizing messages, limiting beliefs, and unfair regulations that impede the work of our social change leaders every single day.

In recent years, society has begun to recognize and attempt to remedy centuries of inequitable and limiting restrictions that we have placed on various groups, including Black and Indigenous people, other people of color, women, and LGBTQ+ folks. These restrictions were based on a fundamental and erroneous assumption that some people are of lesser value than other people.

These inequitable and limiting restrictions have bled into institutions and even whole sectors. Just as we have placed inequitable and limiting restrictions on various groups of people, we have also placed inequitable and limiting restrictions on the social change sector. These restrictions are built upon a similar fundamental and erroneous assumption of lesser value. We have assumed as a society that the social change sector (and those who work within it) are of lesser value than their for-profit counterparts.

Whether you realize it or not, this assumption permeates every aspect of your day-to-day work. From how much money you think you can raise, to how well you take care of yourself and the salary you demand, to whether you ask for help, to how much power you claim—to, ultimately, how able you are to achieve the social change you seek. Consciously or not, we hold down the very sector that can lead the way toward positive social change. So let's escape this dysfunctional system by understanding the various elements that contribute to its dysfunction.

Social Change Work Is Grossly Undervalued

The social change sector's primary role is to make the world a better place. Whether it is alleviating poverty, strengthening democracy, encouraging art and artists to flourish, or creating an equitable educational playing field, the social change sector provides public value. We do this work, stepping in to fix the areas where our systems have failed us, not just because it is the right thing to do, but because we know our economy, society, and planet will be healthier when we all move forward together. The social change sector creates tremendous value for society. But society constantly tells you the opposite.

Worse, you might believe this myth.

Here are a few versions of "you are not worthy" that you may have experienced and internalized over the years:

"Your work is not worthy of significant
money, attention, or time."

"You are not fully competent or efficient."

"You shouldn't have a voice in
politics or policy making."

"You can't be trusted with large sums
of unrestricted money."

"Your work is not as exciting, valuable,
important, or essential as that of businesses."

And my personal favorite:

"You're getting in your own way."

This last one is particularly egregious because it makes it seem as though you, social change leaders, are the source of the problem, when in reality you are simply trying to navigate the obstacles that keep appearing in your path. This is an example of being "gaslighted," a psychological term that refers to the phenomenon when someone manipulates another, perceived as "lesser than," by bombarding them with false information that makes them "doubt... their memory, their perception, and even their sanity" to the point where, over time, they eventually doubt "their sense of identity and self-worth."[1]

I'm not suggesting that we as a society are consciously gaslighting our social change leaders. But we are placing hurdles in your way that make you question your own value and worthiness (and often your own sanity) when the reality is that you are providing tremendous value. Society creates and then feeds a lack of self-belief among our social change leaders, which becomes a self-perpetuating feedback loop.

This dysfunction minimizes social change efforts and ensures that our current inequitable, broken systems stay in place. But you didn't create the many historical, structural, and normative stumbling blocks in your way, and the good news is that once you are aware of them, you can confidently move beyond them.

So, let's start by understanding how our social change system became so broken.

The Sexist Roots of Undervaluing Social Change

The broken system undermining our social change sector did not originate with our current crop of leaders. Understanding this is critical. By becoming aware of that history, and realizing it is just that—*in the past*—you can release the binds that are constricting your social change work.

So let's start at the beginning. Our modern social change sector emerged from a series of eighteenth- and nineteenth-century benevolence movements, through which women who were otherwise kept separate from public life could find a leadership role. These benevolence movements were financially supported by men from the business sector, but led by women. This gendered structure became the precursor to our modern nonprofit sector.[2]

The trend for women to do the "social" work while men paid for it continued into the 1960s and 1970s, when nonprofit leaders were primarily women while business and political leaders were men. The nonprofit organizations of this era were funded by mostly male philanthropists who were happy to provide dollars—as long as those they funded didn't attempt to fundamentally change the underlying system of inequality (through avenues such as political advocacy, for example) from which male-dominated political and financial structures controlled power.[3]

Today not much has changed. Women still make up 75 percent of the nonprofit sector's workforce,[4] while men predominantly control the for-profit and government sectors—men hold 95 percent of the CEO positions at S&P 500 companies,[5] and more than 75 percent of political offices at the state and federal levels.[6] At the same time, the money that funds the nonprofit sector comes largely from the profits of the male-dominated business and government sectors.

Thus the beginnings of our current nonprofit sector were based on an imbalance where men hold financial and political power over women. And here we still largely are. The male-dominated business sector enjoys tremendous riches with which to do their work, while the female-dominated nonprofit sector has to scrape by with limited, and largely funder-restricted, resources. As nonprofit thought leader Kristen Joiner described corporate and foundation funders, "They are looking for the proverbial 'good girl'—an organization that doesn't rock the status quo, that gives them a credential to show they 'care' or 'contribute.'"[7]

Our modern-day social change sector still operates under a dysfunctional dynamic in which nonprofit leaders, who are mostly women, are told by foundations, governments, and corporations led mostly by men—in the regulations and policies they pass, the restricted gifts they donate, and the inadequate fees they pay for services—that they must stay weak, resource-constrained, and subservient.

The Limits of the "Charity" Mindset

From this gendered history of social change, the destructive concept of "charity" emerged, where the *giver* is better and has more power than the *receiver* of aid. "Charity" is a restrictive mindset for both the social change sector and those the sector seeks to serve—instead of viewing the giver of aid and the recipient of aid as equals, charity puts the giver in a position of power over the recipient, and, by extension, the funder of charity in a position of power over the purveyor of charity.

The definition of the word "charity" seems nebulous enough: "generosity and helpfulness especially toward the needy or suffering." [8] But inherent in that is an assumption of inequality between the giver and the receiver. The recipient of "charity" is labeled "needy" and "suffering," rather than empowered—which we all are in reality—to make decisions that direct her own life.

Philanthropy scholar Rob Reich argues that charitable giving is often based on the giver's "judgmental approach to the position of people who are in need and about the things they should be doing differently to lift themselves out of poverty or disadvantage." [9]

Founder of Hull House and beloved early twentieth-century social reformer, Jane Addams, seemingly would agree that how we have approached social change has been a forcing of "our conventions and standards" on those we are attempting to help. Indeed, she argued that "we think much more of what a man *ought* to be than of what he is or of what he may become."[10]

We have structured charity in our society so that the giver forces his ideas and standards on the recipient of the charitable aid. Similarly, the charitable sector—now the nonprofit sector—has been viewed with judgment by those who regulate and fund it, and treated as tangential to and less valuable than the more important "business" sector. As discussed, charity was the purview of the wives who didn't work; as volunteers they devoted their time to helping those in need. But as our social problems became increasingly complex and entrenched, nonprofits began to employ experts—not volunteers—who, through education, knowledge, and experience, knew how to address them.

History is hard to overcome, however, and the expertise of these social change leaders is still often questioned, as their charitable counterparts were. Money given to social change efforts often comes with restrictions on exactly how and when the dollars can be spent, because the underlying assumption is that nonprofit organizations—just like their charitable counterparts—do not have enough expertise or competence to be fully trusted with large, unrestricted sums of money.

At the same time, the approach of charity has always been to assume that the problem lies in the individual recipient of aid, rather than in the overall system. Charity has been about remedying only direct symptoms, not the larger social problem. It has been about feeding, sheltering, and clothing those who don't have enough. Charity has been kept small so that it does not have the power to question or undermine the overall system of wealth inequality in which it operates.

For all of these reasons, the charity mindset can be terribly limiting. In fact, it sidelines and impoverishes the critical work of social change. We must shift from seeking "charity" to integrating social change into everything we do—and that includes within the social change sector itself.

When we stop approaching the work of social change as "charity," we start demanding and creating significant investment, attention, and effort, resulting in actual change to broken systems. And we do that by understanding the work of the social change sector as equal to and fully integrated with the rest of our society and economy.

The Unequal Value Placed on America's Three Sectors

According to the U.S. Bureau of Labor Statistics, in 2018 nonprofits employed 12.3 million people, or more than 10 percent of America's private workforce—more than those of most other U.S. industries, including construction, transportation, and finance.[11] And according to the National Council of Nonprofits, between 2000 and 2016, the number of 501(c)(3) nonprofits in the U.S. increased by almost 75 percent to over 1.4 million.[12] Nonprofits are a significant and critical part of the overall U.S. economy. In fact, they make up one of the

When we stop approaching the work of social change as "charity," we start demanding and creating significant investment, attention, and effort, resulting in actual change to broken systems.

three main sectors of American society, each of which has value and its own unique benefits to society.[13]

The public (or government) sector

This sector is made up of local, state, regional, and national government agencies. Its primary role is to maintain law and order. The public sector's critical assets include political and regulatory powers, large investments in public goods (space exploration, scientific research, transportation infrastructure), the social safety net, and access to most of the population through various distribution channels (taxing authority, census).

The private (or business) sector

This sector is made up of for-profit entities ranging from small family businesses all the way to massive, global corporations. The primary role of this sector is to create financial value, or "wealth." This sector's key assets include flexibility, financial resources, and an ability to innovate for short-term profit.

The social change sector

This sector is made up of nonprofit and philanthropic organizations that serve a "charitable" purpose, as defined by the IRS. I would also include for-profit businesses that have an equally important social purpose (social enterprises). The primary role of this sector is to create social value. The assets of this sector include the abilities to integrate marginalized members of society and to push for change to outdated social structures and norms (social and political reform movements).

ALTHOUGH EACH of these three sectors brings valuable assets to our society, we don't treat them as equals. You could argue that over the past several decades the private sector has increasingly been seen as the most important part of our society. A hubris has grown up around the private sector. As an example, *Forbes* and *Inc.* magazines regularly run articles encouraging nonprofits to "operate like a business"[14] or "run like an innovative business."[15] The advice often follows a similar pattern, drawing on the intelligence and insights of what the writers view as the smarter, more savvy business sector—the CEOs of America's largest corporations are often heralded as geniuses, the most successful startups as heroes.

But, rather than being secondary to other sectors, the social change sector has traditionally played the essential role of filling the gaps left by the other two sectors. Nonprofits often supplement the government's social safety net, and, since the 1960s, government has increasingly relied on the nonprofit sector to provide those social services.[16] Meanwhile nonprofits are often created to address a failure or excess of the private sector, like cleaning up pollution caused by oil companies or alleviating the effects of growing wealth inequality caused, in large part, by decreasing workers' wages and the ballooning wealth of corporate leaders, to name just two.

As government budgets continue to shrink and the wealth of the private sector grows, more and more is being asked of the social change sector. Society increasingly looks to the social change sector not only to provide basic services, but also to solve the mounting social problems facing our world: from inadequate education systems to health care gaps, from growing poverty to racial inequity to ... the list goes on.

But a perception that those who have money are somehow more valuable and powerful than those who hope to use that money to create social value pervades the social change sector. That philanthropists, although often incredibly generous and kindhearted people, came into their wealth through a growing inequality in our society is important to remember.

Over the past several decades, wealth that the private sector creates has increasingly been held in the hands of fewer and fewer people. The wealthiest 5 percent of Americans held about 55 percent of all the wealth in the 1970s, and by 2016 that same group held 68 percent of all wealth. The bottom 90 percent of Americans held about 32 percent of wealth in the 1970s, but only 21 percent of the wealth by 2016.[17] That's a striking divergence between those with money and those without.

Some of those with increased wealth give a portion of it back through philanthropy. This was true in the Gilded Age of the late nineteenth century, when corporate titans like the Rockefellers, Carnegies, and Vanderbilts used portions of their wealth to fund foundations and nonprofit efforts, like the Carnegie libraries or the eradication of hookworm by the Rockefeller Foundation. And it is true today, when technology giants like Mark Zuckerberg, Jeff Bezos, and Bill Gates have used a portion of their enormous wealth to fund foundations and nonprofit efforts.

The philanthropy that helps to fund social change work is increasingly a result of this growing wealth inequality. According to a 2018 report from the Institute for Policy Studies, philanthropy in all its forms, from foundations to individuals to donor-advised funds, is increasingly dominated by the wealthy: "Our charitable sector is currently experiencing a transition from broad-based support across a wide range of donors to top-heavy philanthropy increasingly dominated by a small number of very wealthy individuals and foundations."[18]

This is not to say that nonprofit leaders should eschew philanthropy. On the contrary, philanthropy is a key part of the funding puzzle. But philanthropy must be understood as an equal and symbiotic partner in the work of social change. Often the motivation behind philanthropy is to correct the wrong of wealth inequality—from creating equal educational opportunities to reducing poverty and homelessness to addressing racial disparities. But philanthropy needs social change organizations to do the work of addressing inequality just as much as those organizations need philanthropy.

If nonprofit and philanthropic leaders alike can recognize that philanthropic and nonprofit organizations are both critical and equal actors in remedying society's inequities, powerful and game-changing partnerships can emerge.

And in fact, effective solutions to society's problems will only be found when we view all sectors in a symbiotic relationship. Our society and economy need what each sector brings to the table. A more balanced relationship between sectors—the radical idea that the nonprofit, philanthropic, government, and private sectors are and should be treated as equal partners in solving the many problems we face—is required to move toward a more inclusive, equitable, and healthy society.

Unfair Rules Hold Back Social Change

But we are far from there yet. In fact, we hold the social change sector to a much higher standard than we do the private sector. The sector suffers from a long list of admonitions—real or perceived norms and rules that nonprofits must follow, while businesses enjoy freedom from these often debilitating restrictions. These unfair norms and rules are limiting beliefs in the truest sense because they ultimately limit the reach, sustainability, and effectiveness of social change work.

Here are just a few of the inequitable limitations forced on the social change sector.

Nonprofits must limit political activity more than businesses do

Per federal law, the largest group of nonprofits, 501(c)(3) organizations, must limit their lobbying to an IRS determination that "no substantial part" of the nonprofit's activities include lobbying,[19] whereas, in 2016, the U.S. Chamber of Commerce reported 158 registered business spending more than $100 million on lobbying.[20] Although many nonprofit thought leaders are valiantly trying to educate nonprofit leaders about what they are legally able to do in the realm of political pressure,[21] the vast majority of nonprofit leaders limit their political voices when their business counterparts have free rein to influence public policy to their own gain.

Nonprofits should keep overhead lower than businesses do

For years nonprofits have been counseled to keep the amount of their budget they spend on "overhead" (fundraising and administrative costs) under 20 percent, regardless of their business model. And government funders often require the nonprofits they fund to limit overhead even further, to 10 percent or less. This is referred to as "the overhead myth" in the sector. But according to a report by The Bridgespan Group analyzing the overhead rates of s&p 500 companies, consumer staple companies have a median indirect cost rate of 34 percent, and information technology companies reach a staggering 78 percent.[22] So, we force an arbitrary and impairing overhead rate on nonprofits, while business overhead rates can soar. In recent years some social change sector leaders have attempted to change norms around overhead rates to some positive effect,[23] but the overhead myth still largely remains.

Nonprofits should keep costs lower than businesses do

In almost every aspect, nonprofits are told to keep every expense as low as possible, while businesses have no such restrictions. The most obvious example that I have seen is the boardroom. Nonprofit boardrooms are often windowless, with mismatched or broken chairs and outdated technology, offering lunch sandwiches served in cardboard boxes from the cheapest deli around the corner. Corporate boardrooms enjoy walls of windows with amazing views, designer chairs, state-of-the-art technology, and catered lunches served on china plates. And that is merely one aspect of the unequal day-to-day life enjoyed by a corporation versus a nonprofit.

Nonprofits should hold fewer reserves than businesses do

Operating cash reserves are critical to any organization's ability to plan for the future, innovate, conduct program research and development, and stay afloat during financial downturns. This is true for both nonprofit and for-profit entities. Yet a fairly common belief is that nonprofits should hold few reserve funds so that as much money as possible can be plowed into programs.[24] And according to the Nonprofit Finance Fund's State of the Nonprofit Sector Survey 2018, 50 percent of responding nonprofits had three months or less of operating cash on hand.[25] But companies often enjoy enormous cash reserves, and the security and flexibility that comes from them. In 2019, cash reserves topped hundreds of billions of dollars for our largest corporations.[26]

Far fewer nonprofits than businesses receive large investments

In 2019, only ten nonprofits received gifts of over $100 million (most of these were to large universities or health care institutions).[27] But that's tiny compared to the business sector where, just in the technology space alone, 500 startup companies each received $100 million or more in investments in 2018.[28] Nonprofits are often doing huge work—shoring up crumbling institutions, mending social safety nets, fixing inequitable systems—with nothing close to the requisite financial backing.

THE BOTTOM line is that we, as a society, believe that nonprofits should be managed, regulated, and funded in much more restrictive ways than businesses. And when you, as a social changemaker, subscribe to these limiting beliefs, you and your work are hamstrung.

Release Yourself from This Broken System

Because of these historical, normative, and structural limitations, an overwhelming feeling of scarcity pervades the social change sector. Nonprofit leaders and funders alike believe that there simply is "never enough." There is never enough money, time, talent, influence, people—you name it.

But that feeling of scarcity is simply a mindset, built upon the restrictions nonprofits face at seemingly every turn. The good news is that when you recognize that those limitations are merely a result of the broken system of social change, you can overcome that mindset.

In the social change sector, just as in the rest of our society, we are beginning to recognize that we've been suffering from an inequitable balance of power. Indeed, I believe, as others do, that we are in a time of transfer of power.[29] Society is recognizing a need to move from white, male-dominated power to power that is shared equally by all. I believe that the nonprofit sector, whose historical roots are based in the underlying sexism of our society, is also in the midst of a similar transition.

And you, dear social change leader, are helping to usher in this transition period. Your decision to reclaim your power as an equal partner to funders, board members, policymakers, influencers, and decision-makers can be transformative. Not just for you and your organization's mission, but for our world.

The constraints of scarcity, of sexism, of limiting beliefs are yours to release. Once you fully see this outdated, debilitating system for what it truly is, you can decide if you want to continue to participate in it.

Why do I leave the responsibility for overcoming this dysfunction in the hands of individual social change leaders like you? After all, the overall system is broken. Shouldn't philanthropists and CEOs fix this problem, or at least share an equal responsibility?

My answer is simple. In any system, those with the power have less incentive to change that system. Change to broken systems has only ever happened when individual leaders, who themselves suffered from that broken system, began refusing to continue playing by outdated rules. This is how we outlawed slavery, gave women the vote, and legalized gay marriage. By individuals standing up and saying, "No more!" Those brave souls paved the way for others, and slowly but surely change happened.

I am asking you to stand up and be one of those leaders. We can overcome the dysfunctional system when you and many others refuse to play by these tired rules. And you'll find that when you break those rules, the work becomes easier, more joyful, and even more fun. (Imagine!)

So, the challenge is to fully uncover the limiting beliefs, and then let them go. Once you do, you will realize the tremendous power you have always held inside you.

In the chapters that follow, I will help you move beyond this broken system and open yourself and your organization to the abundance of money, people, and networks that will allow you to realize your social change vision.

Reclaim
Your Power

2

"We are so much more likely to think of the reasons why we we're not right for the job … whatever the excuses are that keep us from being able to raise our hand and say: 'I Am Going to Lead. I Am Going to Lead. I Am Going to Lead.' Because that's what this moment calls for. Because someone has to Lead."

AMERICA FERRERA

HAVE A SECRET. You may not believe it. I didn't believe it when I first encountered it. But I promise you—it is so very true. My secret is this:

You are powerful beyond measure.

You have inside you all the power you need to achieve the social change you seek. All you need to do is step into that power.

Thanks to the broken system of social change we discussed in the previous chapter, you, as a social changemaker, have been told over and over again that you are not valuable enough, not worthy enough, not competent enough. And you have likely allowed these messages to strip you of your own power.

Yep, that's right. I said you gave away your own power. That might be hard to hear. You might vehemently disagree. Or it might make you really mad—at your board, your funders, your staff, your family, yourself, even me. That's okay. Get mad; get furious. Throw this book across the room. It's okay, the book can likely take it. So can I.

Then get quiet. Ask yourself if there might be a kernel of truth somewhere here. Is it possible that you have given away power that you didn't even know you had? That's okay, too. We all do it.

We are all, every single one of us, terrified. Artists, millionaires, politicians, celebrities, authors, singers, leaders, consultants—all of us feel, at some point in our lives, like the world's biggest impostor, that we don't have a clue what we are doing, that we are simply not cut out for the work. Every single one of us doubts ourselves in small and big ways. And in doubting, we give away our own power.

But you have the opportunity to create a different reality. Once you accept that you are giving away your power, you have two choices: work within the confines of the broken social change system and lose sight of the change you are desperately trying to bring to this world; or stand up and say, "Nope. I'm not doing that anymore. My work is too important."

In choosing to say "no!" to this broken system, you are reclaiming your power. I'm not saying it's smooth sailing after that. But with your inner engine pumping at full steam, you are so much more likely to get where you want to go. And, oh yeah, achieve the social change you are working toward, too. All while (bonus!) having so much more fun.

What Is Power?

First, let's look at how power works in organizations like yours. In the 1950s two social psychologists, John R.P. French and

Bertram Raven, defined a new way to think about power.[1] They classified six types of power that individuals can have over others:

- Reward power comes from an ability to give rewards.

- Coercive power stems from an ability to exact punishments.

- Referent power comes from an ability to make others want to model one's own behavior.

- Legitimate power stems from an official title or role.

- Expert power comes from specific and unique expertise.

- Informational power stems from access to specific content or information.

I have seen social change leaders give away their own power too many times to count. You might be giving your power away to:

- a funder, who you feel has reward power over you;

- a government regulator, who you think has coercive power over you;

- a board member, who you believe has legitimate power over you;

- a corporate leader, who you think has expert power over you.

But, in reality, a social change leader—just like any of us— has the opportunity to claim any of kind of power. It is simply a question of deciding to do it.

Recently I was coaching an executive director named Minerva, who leads a cultural arts organization in California. Minerva was frustrated with her board of directors. Her organization's funding and membership numbers were declining, so she desperately needed new board members who could connect the organization to new and bigger networks, offer ideas and expertise around growth, and provide the confidence to lead a bigger strategy. She had repeatedly tried to engage her current board members in recruiting new members, but they were dragging their feet. Minerva complained to me: "I don't know what to do with these board members. We've had meeting after meeting where I try to get them to take action on growing the board. They are incapable of coming up with new ideas and refuse to network and brainstorm names. They have done nothing to recruit new people to the board. I'm so frustrated."

I understand her frustration because I see nonprofit leaders' frustration with unproductive board members all the time. But what Minerva didn't realize is that she had the power to change. Rather than continue to beat her head against the wall of her board members' inaction, she herself could simply recruit her ideal board members. When I suggested this to her, she looked at me incredulously and said, "I can do that?"

Yes, you absolutely can. Because that's what a leader does—uses whatever power at her disposal (expertise, persuasion, action) to achieve something bigger. Obviously no one else in her organization sees the urgency of new board members as well as Minerva does, so she needs to reclaim her power and *lead* the organization where she knows it needs to go. Minerva and I listed the characteristics of her ideal board members—their skills, experience, and networks. Just creating that list started to excite her. Then we brainstormed people Minerva knew who had some of those characteristics, as well as people who didn't have those characteristics themselves, but might be able to connect her to others who did. Minerva's newfound energy and ideas, and most importantly the knowledge that she had the power to create change, propelled her to grow her board despite the apathy of her current board of directors.

As a social changemaker, by definition you are committed to improving circumstances for others. In essence, you are committed to increasing other people's power. That is noble, to be sure, and necessary, but you cannot do that work effectively if you have not found your own power first. Vulnerability and leadership researcher Brené Brown argues that we cannot create better conditions for others until we have found those for ourselves first: "We can't give people what we don't have. We can't fight for what's not in our hearts."[2]

You can't lead social change that seeks to empower the powerless, give voice to the voiceless, make equal the unequal if you haven't first claimed your own power, your own voice, your own equality. Let me show you some ways to get there.

Secure Your Own Mask First

My guess is that if you are leading a social change effort, you have likely been denying your own needs, and thus your own power, for far too long.

I have found that the people attracted to the social change sector tend to be so concerned about their fellow humans that they more often than not put others' needs ahead of their own. Ah, you sweet, loving social change warriors. You are among the most selfless, empathetic people on the planet.

But that empathy can have a sinister side. You may be an over-giver. Giving can only be truly effective when the giver comes from a healthy, wholly fulfilled place.

Psychology Today distinguishes between healthy, generous giving and dysfunctional over-giving. When you give generously, your own needs are fully met and your heart is full. Over-giving, however, comes from "an inability to receive." Over-givers give not because their hearts are overflowing, but rather because they want (or need) something from the recipient of their gifts—appreciation, acceptance, release of an obligation. That is dysfunctional giving. Giving and receiving are meant to be balanced acts. You receive until you are full, and then you give from that place of satiety. If you are unable to fully receive from others, then you are likely giving from "an empty heart." [3]

Being an over-giver is not a good thing. It can be debilitating, and it most certainly strips you of your power. I know you don't want to hear this—I struggled to accept it for years—but you have to fully take care of yourself before you can be of any use to others. You can give something of value to others only when your own bucket is so full that it is overflowing. If you are exhausted, you must rest before you can do that next critically important thing. If you are burned-out, you must create space and time to be inspired again before you can hope to inspire others.

And I am not talking about the fleeting idea of "self-care" that encourages a massage now and again or occasionally turning off your phone. I'm talking about *always* putting your own individual needs ahead of everyone else's—your spouse or partner, your children, your clients, your staff, your board members, your boss, your funders. In securing your own oxygen mask first, you ensure that you have more than enough before you start giving to another.

This is heresy, I know. The idea that you as a social change leader must fully give to yourself before you can give to another is anathema to the culture of a sector steeped in selflessness, martyrdom, and (oh, yeah) dysfunction. Remember the last chapter? If you want to chart a better, more sustainable, more effective future, you have to do things very differently. And a big piece of that is no longer sacrificing your own needs.

So, the next time your staff or your board or your funder or your partner or your child demands something of you, stop and assess. Here's a reminder of your very human needs, and their impact on your work and overall life and happiness, in case you, like so many social change leaders I know, forget what they are.[4]

Physiological needs (air, water, food, sleep)

I can't tell you how many meetings I've been in with a social change leader who had skipped her last meal and hadn't gone to the bathroom for hours because she was just "too busy." This denies your body's very basic needs, and it isn't sustainable. But more importantly, you are sending a very clear message—to yourself and to your observant staff—that *your own body* is less important than pretty much everything else. That's demoralizing and disempowering—and unhealthy.

Safety needs (health, security, property)

As an extension of not taking care of basic bodily needs, social change leaders are also exceptional at denying their overall health and safety, such as by skipping doctor's appointments, not taking vacation time, and ignoring chronic health issues. You have the right to make yourself feel healthy, safe, and secure every day of the week, whatever that looks like for you.

Love and belonging needs (friends, family, connection)

Social change leaders tend to isolate themselves, believing the burden is largely on their shoulders alone. In so doing, they remove themselves from the tremendous support that their surrounding friends, family, peers, and colleagues could offer. But building and cultivating those support networks takes time and space. If you always prioritize work over friends and family, you deny yourself what you need to make those connections, refusing your own fundamental need to love and be loved.

Esteem needs (respect, self-esteem, recognition, strength, freedom)

We all have a need to feel our own power, to believe in ourselves, and to experience the freedom that comes from that. When you strip yourself of your own power and strength, you deny this key aspect of your humanness. When you internalize the messages you've heard for years—that you and your work are not worthy—you ignore your fundamental need for respect.

Self-actualization needs (realizing personal potential, self-fulfillment, personal growth)

The final need we all have is to be fully ourselves—whatever we were put on this earth to do and to be. When you deny yourself, your needs, and your power, you ultimately are denying what you were put here to do. You are denying your own innate desire to be all that you can be, and you are robbing us of the unique gifts you have to offer.

RECENTLY I was coaching one of my clients, Pamela, the CEO of a national foundation, about how to find time in her calendar for rest and relaxation. As we talked, she suddenly started crying. She was shocked by her emotional reaction to what she thought was a logistical conversation but wasn't ready to explore it in the moment. So, I encouraged her to examine her emotional response by writing it out—sitting in a quiet place with pen and paper or laptop and analyzing what she had been thinking and feeling when we discussed her calendar. Pamela later told me that she realized the emotion came from finally seeing how poorly she had been treating herself. She felt true grief for undervaluing the most important person in her life.

Take a hard look in the mirror. Are you acting as if you are not worthy of your own very human needs? My guess is you are.

Let's talk about how you reconnect with your own needs so that when you attack your social change work, you will be doing so from a place of wholeness and centeredness—a place of power.

Find Your Own Brand of Joy

Believe it or not, joy is a fabulous GPS to take you to your power. Because what brings you true joy is a pretty good indicator of the work you are meant to do. Bonus: the work is *infinitely easier* if there is joy in it. I bet that when you started this work, you felt tremendous joy, passion, and inspiration. So what happened along the way?

Try this. Close your eyes for a minute. Take a deep breath, all the way down to below your belly button. Then ask yourself:

"What would my work look like if it were
joyful, passionate, inspiring again?"

Think about what your daily experience of your job would feel like. In case you are struggling for an answer, here are some possibilities:

- You jump out of bed every morning because you are *so excited* to get to work.

- You feel incredibly grateful at various points throughout the day because you get to do this work.

- When you think about your staff and your board, a huge smile breaks across your face because they are so amazing.

- You can easily visualize all of your organization's big goals coming to fruition.

- When you encounter a challenge in the work, you see it as a fun and exciting opportunity to think about how to do things differently and better.

- You take most evening and weekends off because you fully trust that the work that needs doing will be completed within work hours.

- You feel wholly balanced and fulfilled as a human being, and your interests and relationships outside work are flourishing.

Be honest: did you scoff at any of the items on this list? Or did any of them make you feel sad or hopeless? If you had a negative reaction to any, my guess is that you don't have a lot of joy in your job. And you are not alone. In our society, and in the social change sector in particular, we are taught to eschew joy in favor of good, honest, hard work. Social changemakers tend to be some of the most serious people I have ever met. And that makes sense: you carry a heavy burden, and often you are witness to some of the worst suffering in the world. But social change work doesn't need to be joyless. You will be so much more effective at achieving the goals of your job and the larger social change goals of your organization if you are joyful in the work. By tapping into your joy, you reclaim your power.

If you simply cannot find any joy in what you are doing, one of two things might be happening. You may be completely exhausted and burned-out. Or you may be in the wrong place. I would put my money on the first, but if it is the second, be honest with yourself and your board and find a new organization or position that does bring you joy.

If you are simply exhausted, become militant in your pursuit of joy. I read a fabulous article a couple of years ago about a young man named Rodney Smith Jr. who goes around mowing lawns for people because he finds pure joy in the activity. He eventually launched a nonprofit that mows lawns for people all across America.[5] Rodney's story perfectly illustrates that we each uniquely love what we love; we each uniquely find our joy. Mowing lawns isn't very high on my list, but it brings Rodney pure happiness.

Your joy is yours alone, so it's yours to find. But you may be like so many leaders I know and not have a clue what brings you joy. I'm not judging you, because I have been there. There was a time, dear reader, not so long ago, when I had absolutely no idea what to do with a spare hour of time when it materialized. After sitting uncomfortably for fifteen or so minutes, I usually defaulted to doing household chores.

But I learned, over time, that when I connect with what brings me joy (my daily walk in nature, writing in my journal, dinner with my family, a great novel, or a cuddle with my cat, for example) I can feel my inner power light up. Joy gives you so much energy, passion, and drive. It enables you to keep going, and reacquaints you with who you are deep down.

Your center is the core of your being—your gut, your inner knowing, your intuition—whatever you want to call it. It is that place inside you where a deeper knowledge of who you are and your right path exists. You find your center by creating a regular space by yourself.

By "space," I don't mean an afternoon off or a weekend without checking email. I mean time every day when you are beholden to no one, when you have no distractions or demands, when you can just let go. This is where you start to find yourself again—not as a social change leader, but as an individual with interests, passions, and joy. Even if you have small children or other enormous demands on your time, you can find some space. Once you commit to caring for yourself, creative ideas for how you carve out that time (maybe it's bartering childcare duties with a neighbor or getting up before your charges awake in the morning) will come to you. The way back to your center will be uniquely your own, but typically it involves three key steps.

Create space and quiet

Social change leaders are great at filling their lives so incredibly full that they never leave space for time alone. But it is in the quiet by yourself—away from the constant demands of staff, board, funders, partners, spouses, children—that you begin to find your joy.

Spend time there most days

Going to your quiet space once a week is not enough; you have to create a habit, which means doing it almost every day. It might just be five minutes right after you get up every morning, or ten minutes in your car before you head into the office. It doesn't matter where or when you do it, but you must do it most days of the week. At first it will feel like a chore; then it will become a necessity and one of the best parts of your day or week.

Listen to and follow what emerges

The reason to find your quiet space most days of the week is that joy can be shy. You need to regularly provide a place for your joy to emerge and take root. Gradually, you'll get a spark of an idea for what might bring you joy. When you get those sparks, write them down and follow where they lead. I keep a three-by-five-inch inspiration notebook in my purse, and whenever inspiration strikes (a fun activity to do, a topic to explore, a person to call) I write it down. When you listen to your joy, it will emerge stronger and more bountiful. The key is to find the place where you can fairly easily turn off your chatty monkey brain and allow your quiet, inner knowing to emerge.

WHEN I met Samira, a program officer for a national education-related foundation, she had strayed far from her joy. Samira had entered the education arena many years ago as a bright, engaging high school English teacher. She loved the work, her students, and making a difference in her students' lives (although as a humble person, she would never openly admit the impact she had). Because she was such a great teacher, she caught the eye of a national foundation and was offered an opportunity to steward a portfolio of education reform efforts. She was initially thrilled by the job and brought her usual energy to the position. But over several years, she became increasingly beaten down by the bureaucracy within the foundation. Her great ideas were thwarted by her boss, the board, the legal team, or the foundation's policies. She also worked a grueling schedule that gave her scant time to hit the restroom between meetings, let alone time to think. Day after day, Samira's joy faded and, not surprisingly, so too did her ability to effectively help her education grantees.

Samira and I worked to tap back into her joy—where her true power to create social change lay. We first figured out ways to release her from the day-to-day overwhelm of the position. We set up a system for delegating or off-loading tasks to others so that she could focus on the tasks that gave her energy while carving out time every day to go for a hike or sit quietly with her coffee—Samira's personal brand of joy. Then we began talking about projects that inspired her. The more we talked, the more ideas and energy sparked in Samira. Once we found that energy again, we developed ways for her to scale the various obstacles her foundation put in her path—from changing the energy of the boardroom to using an abundance worldview (which we'll discuss in chapter three) to overcoming others' objections. Over time, Samira reclaimed her joy—and her power to create social change.

In our increasingly "always-on" world, you will be so much more powerful if you regularly find time to reconnect with your center. From that place of connection to your joy and your center, powerful action can emerge. In your effort to achieve your mission, imagine how the tide might shift if you regularly stepped away from the noise and acted from a place of quiet, connection, and courage: Instead of reacting to the tumult, you become silent and truly listen, to understand what your gut is telling you to do. A quiet, thoughtful approach allows you to move from *reacting to* circumstances to *creating* them.

An added benefit to finding your center and following your joy on a fairly regular basis is that your self-doubt will begin to melt away. If you have nicely paved a road to your own inner knowing, when someone questions one of your decisions, you can easily (and sometimes in the moment) check in with your gut to see if that dissenting opinion has merit. You will no longer be swept away by the most recent person or opinion that holds sway over you.

From the quiet of your center, you will be much better positioned to build an effective organization, create smart strategies, develop deep networks, and attract ample resources. You will be better able to focus on what fuels you so that you are refreshed each day to start anew. In listening to yourself you ensure that, each day, you have the energy, the optimism—the power—necessary to see your social change goals realized.

Claim Your Value

Once you start hanging out in your center more often you will begin to realize that you, and your work, are incredibly valuable. As I discussed in the previous chapter, the dysfunctions of the social change sector have likely kept you from recognizing the tremendous value that you and your organization are providing your clients, your community, and our world.

One of the things I love about social changemakers is that you are such a selfless bunch. My guess is that you are uncomfortable acknowledging the pivotal role you play in your organization. But as the leader of your staff, your board, and even the funders, volunteers, and clients you assemble, you play an absolutely pivotal role. Without you pointing the way and marshalling everyone and everything in the right direction, all would be lost.

Here's the thing: The social change you work so tirelessly to achieve is more likely to happen if you fully recognize and assert your value and your organization's value.

One obvious way that social change leaders fail to recognize their value is in not demanding to be paid what they are truly worth. I saw the most blatant example of this at a conference recently, when I met a nonprofit leader named Patricia, the leader of a national organization aimed at helping more people of color become political leaders. She has an amazing, inspiring vision for the required change, critical data about what works and what doesn't, and a clear, articulate plan for how to make change a reality. I was blown away by her solution to make racial equity in leadership a reality. When I told her this, she said, "If only I could grow my solution to more places." Since I know that the hurdle to growth in the social change sector is almost always money, I asked her about her organizational budget. She replied, in a small, embarrassed voice, "I have no money to hire a staff, and I decided a year ago to give up my own salary. I just can't raise money for this." So, she is trying to grow this amazing platform for racial equity on pennies—literally.

Patricia thought the problem was that she couldn't raise money. But the real problem is that she doesn't value herself or the solution she has to offer enough to demand sufficient financial investment. She completely stripped the worth from herself, her organization, and her social change goals before she had even left the gate. When she decided to create a budget that didn't include salaries for her and some staff, she signaled to the world that her ideas have little value. She told any potential funder that her time had no dollar value. Funders, and the world, reacted accordingly. Patricia is unwittingly sinking her critically important work.

The solution for Patricia is to create a realistic budget for how much it costs to create the social change she envisions,

The social change you
work so tirelessly to achieve
is more likely to happen if
you fully recognize and
assert your value and your
organization's value.

and then start meeting with funders whom she knows, whom her board knows, and show them what she has already done and what it will cost to do much more.

You may argue that Patricia's problem was a lack of access to people with money. But the conference where I met Patricia was hosted by one of the largest national foundations. They specifically invited Patricia to present because they were so blown away by her work. But they, mistakenly, thought that Patricia had all the money she needed.

There are so many ways, big and small, that social change leaders undervalue themselves and their work. To truly claim your and your organization's value, stop acting like a charity and start investing in the things that would make the work easier, more enjoyable, more joyful.

Ask yourself, every day:

"What would make the work easier and more joyful?"

What you come up with will be uniquely yours because, as I've said, joy is uniquely yours to find, but a few ideas to get you started might include:

- paying yourself and your staff higher salaries;
- upgrading your technology;
- not working on most weekends;
- finding brighter, more efficient office space;
- purchasing nicer food at your meetings and events.

These things all cost money. So, you may think that I've created a catch-22 because you need to first have money to spend money in ways that demonstrate your value. But often in the simple act of claiming your own value, the world around you starts responding in kind, and money and abundance start to flow. I get how hard that is for you to believe, so stick with me because in the coming pages we will talk about how to raise money for the things that will make you feel more valued. First, treat yourself, your staff, and your organization in ways that make you feel valued, joyful, and energized. Abundance will follow.

This shift—in claiming her own value and welcoming abundance—happened for one of my clients. Judy runs a nonprofit that creates greater equity in K–12 public education. Her programs have a long track record of closing the academic achievement gap between students of diverse backgrounds. Her programs successfully increase student academic performance, and thus save school districts millions of dollars—by decreasing expenses that would otherwise have been spent on academic interventions and additional teachers, and increasing revenue when fewer students drop out of school.

However, Judy's nonprofit had never received money from the school districts in which her organization worked. Her staff had, for years, privately fundraised for the costs of their programs. Judy was fed up with not being paid by the school districts for services that provided them tremendous value. I encouraged her to research how much money her nonprofit was saving school districts and how much school districts were investing in other (inferior) programs.

I helped her put together a confident presentation that demonstrated all this for the superintendent of her largest school district. In the meeting, Judy argued that the school district should provide an annual portion of the program costs. The superintendent was so wowed by the argument that she agreed. For the first time in its history, the superintendent included significant, multiyear support for Judy's program in the district budget. Thus emboldened, Judy restructured the agreements with her other school districts to model this new cost-sharing approach. Since then, school districts have funded more than a third of Judy's annual budget, when they used to fund none of it.

Judy could have simply swallowed the fact that school district leadership didn't value the services her nonprofit provided. But instead she pointed out the disconnect between the value her nonprofit provided and the money the school districts invested, and stood up for her organization. Judy reclaimed her, and her nonprofit's, power—and abundance followed.

Ask for Help

In beginning to see your value, it becomes easier to ask for the help I know you desperately need. Because (and I know this will be a shock to many of you) it's not all up to you.

Let that just sink in for a second:

It is NOT all up to you.

See if this reminds you of anyone: One of my clients, Vivian, the leader of a national homeless and housing non-profit, used to stay up until midnight most nights dealing with administrative tedium (scheduling travel and meetings, responding to emails, writing reports, filing) because she refused to hire an executive assistant. During board meetings she took on most, if not all, action items because she doubted anyone else would. In staff meetings she often shifted tasks from other people's lists to hers because she knew how over-worked her staff was. Sound familiar?

The sad part is that Vivian is the norm, not the exception. I see so many social change leaders take on much more than they have the capacity to do. Instead of giving 100 percent effort, it's as if social change leaders feel that anything less than 250 percent is unacceptable. The end result for so many of these leaders, and for Vivian when she found her way to me, is that they are exhausted, burned-out, sick, defeated, or all of the above. The even sadder part is that working past your 100 percent has diminishing returns. When you work beyond your capacity, you accomplish less than you would if you had stopped sooner.

The solution I offered Vivian, and that I offer you, is to figure out where your 100 percent effort lies, and stop there. Then determine how to delegate, outsource, ask for help, or simply not do the rest.

So, how do you figure out your 100 percent? Your 100 percent is the work that feels joyful, effortless, energizing. Your 100 percent ends when the work in front of you suddenly feels draining or hard.

As you go through your daily tasks, pay attention to your energy level. As soon as you cross over into feeling tired or drained, it is a clue that you have strayed past your 100 percent. This concept is so hard for selfless social change leaders to hear, but you are doing harm to your organization, and more importantly to yourself, once you pass the 100 percent threshold. Because once past it, your energy, your drive, your excitement, your ability to attract, inspire, and mobilize the armies of people you need behind you greatly diminishes.

We are energetic beings. Therefore, the energy we bring to any endeavor is everything. If you are bringing exhausted, frustrated, anxious energy to the work, you are setting your organization up for failure. You will be infinitely more powerful if, when the work starts to feel hard, you rest and reconnect with your center and your joy until you feel energized to take up the work again.

"*But hold on!*" I can hear you screaming. "There is so much work to do. How can I possibly just stop doing it if I'm not excellent at it, or when it feels hard or joyless? I don't have that luxury!"

I hear you. But the truth is that you are infinitely more powerful when you recognize what you do and don't do well. One way to think about this is by mapping all your tasks to their zones of competence. Gay Hendricks developed this system for figuring out where to focus your efforts. There are four zones:[6]

- **Zone of incompetence (I).** These are the tasks you are just not good at, and consequently they are likely also the tasks that are not fun for you. Don't worry, we all have zones of incompetence.

- **Zone of competence (C).** You are capable and efficient at these activities, but a lot of other people are as well. These tasks also likely don't bring you joy.

- **Zone of excellence (E).** You are expert at these activities because you have honed these skills over many years, through education and/or experience. Because you are good at them, they are probably fun and easy for you.

- **Zone of genius (G).** This is where the magic happens. You do these activities better than the vast majority of people because they are within your unique, natural-born abilities. Because you were born to do these tasks, they are incredibly easy and joyful for you. This is your sweet spot, so you want to spend the vast majority of your time here.

Typically the tasks of a social change leader fall into roughly some of these categories (or most of them, if you lead a tiny organization and have few staff or volunteers):

- board development and management,
- staff development and management,
- organizational strategy,
- program delivery,
- financial management,
- fundraising,
- external partnership/network building,
- marketing and communications,
- thought leadership,
- influencing policy/lobbying/education,
- volunteer engagement and management.

List all the activities you currently do in each of these applicable categories. Then review that list of tasks and label each according to its applicable zone by honestly asking yourself:

"Am I unskilled at this task (I),
relatively good at it (C),
excellent at it (E), or
born to do it (G)?"

The items that fall into your zone of excellence and zone of genius are where to focus your time. You have no business doing the tasks that fall into your zones of incompetence and competence, since you either are doing harm (zone of incompetence), or you are adequate at them but many other people could take those items off your list (zone of competence). That's when you outsource or simply eliminate that work. And, as I've said, your zones of incompetence and competence don't bring you joy.

If you are going to stop doing some tasks, then someone else needs to do a whole lot of work, right? So, you must ask for help.

Wait, what? Yep, heresy, I know, in the social change sector, which prides itself on cultivating a martyr complex among its leaders. In a sector defined by doing more with less, the assumption is that social change leaders can rarely afford the help they really need. But think about how harmful this view is.

Every single one of us needs help pretty much every step of the way. We humans are social animals; we know in our bones that we are stronger together. Why would we expect that social changemakers are somehow different?

There is absolutely no shame in admitting that you can't do it all. I'm sorry to tell you, but even though you are an awesome social change warrior, you are not superhuman. You are a regular, ordinary human. And just like the rest of us, *you need help*. You have the right to admit that the work is too hard, or that being a social change leader is lonely. And most importantly, you have the right to raise your hand and ask for someone to help carry the load.

The shocking thing, which I have witnessed more and more in my own life, is that as soon as you request it, help shows up in pretty short order. But you have to be completely open to receiving that help, in whatever form it appears.

That help can come from many sources:

- your board;
- your staff;
- volunteers;
- outside firms (consulting, accounting, marketing, virtual assistance);
- friends and family;
- peers and colleagues;
- collaborators and partners;
- God, the Universe, your guardian angels, if you so believe.

And if you are thinking (because I know you are), "But I don't have the money to get help," save that scarcity thought until the next chapter, where I show you how an abundance approach can solve it.

First, simply recognize that when you ask for help, you will be infinitely more powerful. I grew up in a Catholic household, but as soon as I went to college I left religion behind. It just didn't resonate with me. But what I unknowingly held on to was prayer. Whenever I found myself struggling, confused, or lost I would (almost subconsciously) offer up a prayer—to whom, I didn't really know. But the act of simply saying "I cannot do this alone" was almost always transformative. Admitting that the burden was simply too heavy for me to carry on my own opened me to something or someone else entering in to help shoulder the burden.

That simple act, the act of opening yourself up to receive, is what asking for help ultimately does. Essentially, you give yourself permission to not carry the load alone.

You are the leader of the social change that your organization seeks. A true leader knows that she is most powerful when she focuses on what she does best and then asks for help for the rest.

Cultivate Your Compassion

Asking for help will likely be much easier if you grow compassion for yourself and others. How can compassion be a path to greater power? And aren't social change leaders among the most compassionate people? Indeed, your deep compassion drives you to make the world a better place. Although I don't doubt that you have tremendous compassion for those you serve, you likely lack compassion for some other key people. But if you cultivate your compassion for them as well, you can dramatically grow your power.

First, there is compassion for your board members. Believe me, I know how frustrating board members can be. They can be distracted, distracting, self-involved, meddlesome, or simply *in the way*. You need them to step up to the plate, but they often just don't get it or won't do it. But what if they want to help and are scared of doing the wrong thing or have too much on their plate or don't know how to take the first step? Could you temper your frustration at their ineffectiveness by seeing it as an expression of the human imperfection we all have? When you develop true compassion for your board members, you can approach them with equanimity and brainstorm how to work together more productively.

Even more difficult, but so very important, is growing your compassion for funders. I know how frustrating funders can be. If funders would just step up, make bigger bets, get out of the way, this social change work would be so much easier, right? But what if that foundation program officer is as scared as you are? What if he doesn't have much experience in social change work or has a board and a boss breathing down his neck? What if the head of that government agency is afraid of screwing up or can't figure out how to navigate all the red tape? If you have real compassion for your funders, you can analyze what might be causing the roadblocks and then work with them to find solutions.

Finally, you will find even more solutions for overcoming challenges with your board and your funders by cultivating compassion for yourself. I have come to realize that when we lack self-compassion, we are not fully tapping into our power. But if you can feel true compassion for yourself as an exhausted, tireless, passionate, but flawed (like all humans) leader, you will be transformed.

As a die-hard perfectionist, I've waged a lifelong struggle with self-compassion. Recently, I decided that my own inner critic needed to take a back seat, so I started doing a daily loving-kindness practice, which is a simple way to build compassion. In case you're not familiar with it, the loving-kindness practice is a Buddhist tradition, although it is not inherently religious. It is simply the act of wishing happiness and health first to yourself, then to someone you love, then to an acquaintance, then to someone that you are challenged by, and finally to the entire world. It can take less than five minutes, but the impact is life changing. You can find guided loving-kindness meditations in apps like Insight Timer.

Because, here's the thing: When you let compassion grow, for yourself, for your supporters, and for those you need help from, suddenly you realize that life isn't "me versus them," but "all of us in this together." We all stumble, we all get scared, we all lose our way, and we all sometimes struggle to find the next right step.

And the truly transformative part is that you realize the person you are most critical of (usually yourself) is just as human as the rest of us. When you recognize the humanity and imperfection in those you love, those who challenge you, and especially in yourself—*baby, watch out!*

Elevate Yourself,
Then Lift Up Those Around You

All these avenues to growing your power—finding your joy, claiming your value, asking for help, cultivating compassion—are simply ways of elevating yourself so you can become more of the beautiful, powerful social leader you were meant to be.

Stay with me a minute and try this experiment.

Close your eyes. Visualize some great future event happening to your organization. Picture an enormous check arriving in the mail for more money than you have ever raised. Watch yourself hold the big check in your hands. See your board all around you, smiling and excited, and your staff next to you, energized. Picture your clients supported and transformed. Watch all the hopes you have for your work coming fully to fruition. Just sit in that moment of glory and achievement for a second. Bask in it.

With your eyes still closed, take a deep breath and scan your body from the top of your head, all the way down your torso, down your arms to your fingertips, and down your legs to your toes. What do you notice? Do you sense a tingling, or a pulsing, or a humming? Do you feel energy zinging through you? Do you sense something like maybe joy or peace or contentment moving through your body, however subtly? Just notice how your body feels in that moment of visualizing your nonprofit's future glory. There's no right answer.

Now, open your eyes, take a deep breath, shake out your hands, wiggle your toes.

This stuff is really telling, so stay with me for another minute. Close your eyes again.

This time, think about something very negative happening to your organization. Visualize your entire board resigning, your funding drying up, your staff leaving. See it all happening and be in that horrible moment, just for a second. With your eyes still closed, do another body scan—from the top of your head, down your torso, down your arms to your fingertips, and down your legs to your toes. What do you notice? Do you sense a tense, brittle energy? Do you feel guarded, closed off, protective, tight? Do you sense tension, discomfort or pain in your body? Take a minute and explore how your body feels in that negative moment. Again, there is no right answer.

If you do this exercise, you will likely experience two contrasting forms of energy: a high-powered, exciting, inspiring, light, *propelling* energy in the first exercise; and a dragging, heavy, *debilitating* energy in the second. The energy you project into the world is typically the same kind of energy you attract. If you want to experience more energy that propels you and your organization toward greater heights of success, then spend more time thinking and focusing on energizing, inspiring thoughts. If you'd rather hang out with the heavy, debilitating energy, then spend more time thinking and focusing on fearful, anxiety-producing thoughts.

The choice is yours.

Spending your time in low-energy thoughts like fear, doubt, and anger breeds scarcity, powerlessness, and inertia. But instead finding your joy, claiming your value, asking for help, and cultivating compassion moves you and your work toward abundance and success.

I saw this power of elevating your energy with my client Paul in a recent coaching session. Paul is the executive director of a New York-based arts organization that he started a decade ago to build local support for artists and their work. When I first met Paul, I could tell that he was so mired in the challenges, the fear, the muck that he could not move forward. So I asked him to describe what his ideal organization would look like a year into the future. After a slow, resistant start, Paul began to describe something amazing. He saw a larger, more effective, more engaged board; he saw a bigger staff that freed him up to do more speaking, network building, fundraising; he saw his programs growing to serve more people, more effectively. His spirit started to lift, and I got goosebumps—I could feel the shift in his energy. In that instant he became the leader he wanted to be and the leader his organization desperately needed. I suggested he do that same exercise at least once a day—either writing it out, saying it aloud, or simply closing his eyes and imagining it.

Our imaginations are incredibly powerful, but we discount that. If you start to exist in the world that you want (even if only in your imagination), you will start to believe that it is possible. You will start to exude that powerful, propelling energy, and change will come. It did for Paul, who has just added some fantastic people to both his staff and board, is knocking his fundraising goals out of the park, and has in a few short months started to significantly turn his organization around. Simply because he committed to elevating his own energy.

I'm not suggesting that you fake your feelings. If you are feeling fearful, frustrated, hopeless, experience those feelings. Feel them all the way through and then consciously choose activities that will elevate your energy again.

And the really cool thing is that you can also elevate the energy of others in your organization. Because, again, energy attracts like energy. So, if you enter a room where your staff is complaining about the latest funder hijinks, or your board is worrying about the political climate, or a prospective funder is bemoaning the state of the world, refuse to meet them there. Help them focus on the positive, on the better future, on the amazing solutions your organization offers—on where you're going, not where you've been.

The next time you feel the energy of your staff, your board, your funders, or your partners waning, try one of these elevating statements:

"I agree that this funder is being difficult. Let's brainstorm some things we could do or say to get them to move in a more helpful direction."

"Yes, this is a really challenging political environment, and I get why you are worried about how we move our mission forward in the midst of it, but are there other, apolitical avenues we could pursue in the meantime?"

"I wonder if we are focusing too much on what's not working. Can we take a few minutes to talk about what is working and see if we can apply any learnings from those things to this troubling situation?"

I'm not asking you to be a Pollyanna. When things are challenging or difficult or frustrating, acknowledge it, bemoan it, and then move on. Because if you decide to stay stuck in the muck, that's where you will remain. Lead yourself, and then your staff and board, to acknowledge the brick wall and find a way around it. Use your imaginations to realize the social change you all seek. Trust me, you have the power to change your energy and the energy of those whose help you need.

In elevating your energy, you are ultimately saying "yes!" to your internal power. You are flipping the "on" switch of your own beautiful light. You don't need anyone's permission to be powerful; you already have inside you all the power you could ever need to achieve the social change you seek. You are powerful beyond measure.

So, now that you have elevated your energy, let's attack that biggest of energy suckers in the social change sector: the scarcity mindset.

3

Kiss
Scarcity
Goodbye

"An old friend of Robert Frost's was driving him home on a moonlit August night, with huge stars in the sky. The friend mused, 'On a night like this, I keep thinking that life is so short, and there is so little time.' Frost put a hand on his arm and said, 'It's the other way around, you know. There is so much time. More than anyone could ever need.'"

JAY PARINI

SOCIAL CHANGE LEADERS have been told for so long that they must scrape by, are not worthy of real investment, and deserve only the leftovers—of money, of people, of time. It is no wonder a scarcity mindset—a fundamental belief that there is not enough—pervades the social change sector. There is not enough money, enough funders, enough volunteers, enough board members, enough time, enough political sway, enough influence.

My guess is that you—like most social change leaders and their staffs, board members, and funders—automatically think that there simply is not, and never will be, enough resources for what you ultimately want to accomplish. Scarcity is such a profound psychological impediment, because if your assumption is one of constant deficiency, then there is never any reason to try for more. And thus scarcity becomes your reality. Every single day.

But reality is the other way around, you know. There is so much more than any social change leader could ever need. There is an abundance of supporters, advocates, volunteers, board members, collaborators, partners, experts, influence—even money! This abundance is waiting for you to tap into it. If you start by simply believing that there is enough out there for you and for your social change work, then that belief will propel you forward to meet it. If you decide to switch from a scarcity to an abundance worldview, the sky is the limit.

I saw this with a national membership organization focused on creating a more effective, equitable health care system. Its CEO, Fred, came to me wanting to jump off the hamster wheel of never having enough to achieve the organization's big social change goals. They had spent years either just barely scraping by or having to cut staff because they could not attract enough money.

I started by working with Fred, his staff, and his board to articulate their top priorities as an organization. It turned out they had really big goals—goals that, the more we talked about them, everyone was increasingly excited by. We created a long-term strategy for bringing those big goals to fruition, outlining how much it would cost, and how their financial model needed to change to sustain that growth. With this newfound clarity about their goals for the future and what it would take to make them happen, Fred got several new funders to make large, multiyear investments and attracted new members, while increasing investment from current members. Two years later, they have doubled their budget, grown their staff, increased their membership, and, most importantly, expanded their services and their influence on health care policy.

Fred's organization moved toward abundance the moment they decided that something more was possible. Change like this necessitates a belief that scarcity can be overcome. And it can. But first, let's understand scarcity thinking for what it is.

What Is a Scarcity Mindset?

In the social change sector, scarcity thinking is often referred to as "the starvation cycle" in which nonprofit leaders so often find themselves. This cycle starts when you believe you can't attract enough money, so you skimp on staff and systems, becoming less effective, forcing you to serve fewer clients, resulting in less social change. It is a vicious downward cycle. And it is not just nonprofit leaders who suffer from this scarcity mindset. Funders, both philanthropic and governmental, play an equal role in perpetuating the scarcity mindset.

Ann Goggins Gregory and Don Howard coined the term "starvation cycle" in their pivotal *Stanford Social Innovation Review* article. The article clearly articulates a downward spiral where funders hold "unrealistic expectations" about the true and full costs of the nonprofits they want to support, and then the leaders of those nonprofits feel pressure to meet those unrealistic expectations by spending far too little on fundraising, administration, and infrastructure (what many refer to as "overhead costs"; see the discussion of the overhead myth in chapter one).[1] The end result is that nonprofits are starved of the real and necessary costs of running an effective and sustainable organization. And so, effective and sustainable social change eludes us all.

Even though Goggins Gregory and Howard's article was written more than a decade ago and served as a wake-up call, the social change sector is still firmly entrenched in a scarcity mindset. The belief that resources have always been and will always be scarce pervades everything.

And it's not just a belief that money is scarce. Many scarcity-based beliefs float through the halls of nonprofit and philanthropic organizations. Scarcity thinking essentially means living in the world of lack. Here are some of the "lacks" I've heard social change leaders bemoan, and why these "lacks" are just a chosen viewpoint.

We lack the money to add fundraising staff or systems

Many nonprofit leaders are unwilling to risk hiring a top-notch fundraiser (or securing the best donor database, or revamping their online presence, or investing in other critical fundraising infrastructure) because they don't have the money. But that is a self-perpetuating cycle, because without improving how you raise money, you will never raise more money. If you are unhappy with the amount of money you bring in the door, then you need to change *how* you bring money in the door, and often that requires an upfront investment in people and systems. The adage "it takes money to make money" is as true in the nonprofit sector as it is in the for-profit sector.

We lack the money to pay market rate salaries

Related to this is the nonprofit sector's ever-present fear that there isn't enough money to pay for truly talented staff. Figuring out the market rate for top talent is easy, but overcoming aversions to that dollar figure is tricky. A scarcity mindset solidly sticks you in the position of paying for less-experienced or less-competent staff. You get what you pay for. If you want your nonprofit to knock it out of the park, set salaries that attract top-notch talent and then watch what happens.

We lack the money to pay for high-quality infrastructure and systems

So many nonprofit organizations subsist with outdated technology, cobbled-together systems, and subpar websites, because they (erroneously) believe that they must keep their overhead costs as low as possible and spend as much as possible on their mission. But you simply cannot have a strong mission without spending money on the high-quality systems necessary to run those programs.

We lack the partners or influencers necessary to achieve our mission

Nonprofit leaders often isolate themselves and their organizations from other entities with similar social change goals—those entities they may compete with for limited funds. But if you think of those funding resources as abundant instead of scarce, you can break down your walls and connect with other people, organizations, and networks with similar visions for the future. You can combine your efforts for much larger gains. A networked nonprofit is far better positioned than an isolated, solitary organization to create sustainable social change. (We'll discuss this in greater detail in chapter five).

We lack the power to create policy change

Far too often, social change leaders see scarcity in political power. Since the 2016 election and the resulting and ongoing blows to progressive social change agendas, I have seen some nonprofit leaders bury their heads in the sand, figuring they will wait out these punishing political winds until something better comes along. But if you have a compelling social change vision, you can tap into an abundance of outrage and activity now—in fact, many thought leaders argue that now is the time for nonprofits to embrace their advocacy power.[2] And even if advocacy at the federal level may not make sense for your mission at a certain point in time, there is ample opportunity for affecting policy change at the state and local levels. Research suggests that a state or local strategy is sometimes an easier and more efficient way to change minds and policy. This has been true over time, from women's suffrage to the repeal of prohibition in the 1920s to the legalization of interracial marriage in the 1950s to the legalization of gay marriage in 2015 and more.[3]

We lack the confidence to create a long-term plan

The height of scarcity thinking is when social change leaders create a long-term plan and then make a second plan—the backup plan—for when that first plan falls through. In doing so, you are, right out of the gate, telling yourself and the world that your first plan is sure to fail. When you create a plan B you are in essence saying that you don't fully believe in the viability of the direction and model you just spent months researching, analyzing, and creating. And you are telling your funders, advocates, influencers, staff, board, volunteers, clients, and others standing by ready to help you realize your vision that your organization isn't worthy of that vision. When you create a backup plan, you unnecessarily hinder yourself, your organization, and the great work you can do. Research from the Wisconsin School of Business found that creating a backup plan actually undermines your chances for success.[4]

ALL THESE examples of scarcity thinking in the social change sector demonstrate how destructive this lack-based mindset is to your work and your social change vision. Scarcity thinking insidiously limits you, your organization's work, and the ultimate social change you were put on this earth to achieve. When you fundamentally believe that only pennies are available to you, pennies are all that you will find.

Fear Is Not Your Friend

Scarcity thinking is essentially planting your feet firmly in the land of fear. And indeed, fear is a pervasive energy in the social change sector. But fear is not your friend. Fear strips you of your power. Fear engages the amygdala part of your brain and kicks in your fight, flight, or freeze reflex. And we all know that once it fires up, you have very little true power. Sure, you could probably punch someone in the face, or run farther than you ever have before, but neither of those actions will bring you closer to achieving your mission.

Never let fear make the decisions. Think about it. When you were a child heading off to your dark bedroom, you likely had a palpable fear of the monsters under your bed (or, in my case, monsters in the closet—my bed was really low to the ground, and we all know that monsters are pretty large). When you felt that fear in your chest, or your stomach, or wherever, did you feel powerful? Probably not. You probably wanted to become as small as possible or somehow escape. You were unable to deal rationally with the monster situation. Who among us had the insight to turn the light on, look those monsters in the eye, and yell, "Go away!" Not me, that's for sure.

When you fundamentally believe that only pennies are available to you, pennies are all that you will find.

Maybe you don't want to admit it, but your situation with the countless fears that swirl around you and your organization on any given day is the same. You have to turn the light on, uncover the monsters, and face them head on. Powerfully.

Whenever you feel fear rising up within you (or within your staff, board, funders, or partners), recognize it and name it. Here's where the self-compassion we discussed in chapter two comes in again. We are all scared, every single one of us, most days. Anyone who claims not to be afraid is lying. So, if you are afraid, likely your staff and board are, too. The beauty of naming your fears (fears that others likely share) is that you then know what you are truly dealing with and can work together to move beyond that fear.

The worst thing you can do is to make decisions for your organization when you are in the grips of fear. Fear-based decision making roots your organization and your work squarely in a scarcity mindset. When your choices are driven by fear you send the message—to yourself, your staff, your clients, your board, your funders—that you don't have, you will never have, enough.

If instead you fundamentally believe that endless dollars, people, time, connections, and power are heading your way, then that is what you will discover waiting for you.

Let me show you how.

Abundance Is Out There

More money is out there than you will ever need to achieve your social change goals. As a single but very powerful data point: two hundred–plus mega philanthropists have signed on to Bill Gates's Giving Pledge since 2010, promising to give away more than half of their wealth before they die.[5] But they are largely failing at this. Rather than seeing their wealth decrease since they pledged (because they are giving so much away), many pledgers are witnessing their wealth grow. The starkest example of this is Paul Allen, cofounder of Microsoft and the wealthiest giving pledger. When Allen died in 2018, his net worth was $20 billion, or almost 50 percent more than when he signed the Giving Pledge in 2010.[6] Although he may have wanted to direct $10 billion to the social change sector before he died, he was unable to do so.

We could sit around and argue about why he and the other giving pledgers, who control billions of dollars that could be directed to the social change sector, have failed so miserably at channeling their money there. And many have thoughtfully opined about this.[7]

But, for me, the much more important point is that money exists—so much money, more than any social change organization could ever need. Money that desperately wants to make its way to the sector is not getting there, which means something is blocking that money from reaching its target. So, the bad news is that an enormous amount of money that could be working toward social change is lying dormant; but the good news is that the money exists. You just have to shift your ability to receive it. And you do that by leading yourself, your board, your staff, and your funders from a scarcity to an abundance worldview.

Adopt an Abundance Worldview

The fantastic news is that your ability to attract the abundance out there directly relates to your belief that you can attract it. And your belief comes from how you approach the world.

We can either believe that what we attract and achieve is limited by history (the scarcity worldview) or we can believe that so much more is possible (the abundance worldview).

The abundance worldview is infinitely preferable because it sets you up to do and be so much more—even to achieve the impossible. An abundance worldview means you believe that what you are starting with is just that: a starting point. You can move far beyond that starting point through your efforts. The simple act of embracing an abundance worldview creates momentum and an ability to achieve so much more.

The abundance worldview can be absolutely transformative for the social change you seek. If, rather than being trapped in a scarcity worldview where you automatically assume that resources will always be limited, you instead believe that an abundance—of money, people, power, time—is just waiting to be unlocked by you, then I assure you, you will find it.

If you, like the vast majority of social change leaders, find yourself locked within the omnipresent scarcity worldview, the children's television series *Sesame Street* might be able to help.

In 2014, singer Janelle Monáe performed a song called "The Power of Yet" for the show.[8] The idea behind the song is that when you encounter any lack, just add the word "yet" to it. For example, if you struggle because you aren't good at playing basketball, you can move from scarcity to abundance by adding "yet." So, "I'm not good at basketball" is limiting.

But "I'm not good at basketball, *yet*" is expansive; it's abundant. In an instant, that three-letter word provides a runway to so much more.

So the next time you encounter a lack in your work, add a "yet." Here are a few examples to get you started:

SCARCITY WORLDVIEW	ABUNDANCE WORLDVIEW
We don't have enough money to achieve our goals.	We don't have enough money to achieve our goals, *yet*. But if we put together a smart money-raising plan, we will.
We don't have enough of the right people on our board.	We don't have enough of the right people on our board, *yet*. But we can start brainstorming ideal candidates and then figure out how to connect with them.
We don't know how to fundraise effectively.	We don't know how to fundraise effectively, *yet*. But if we start researching and asking experts for help, we can get much better at it.
We don't have access to the policy influencers necessary to move our mission forward.	We don't have access to the policy influencers necessary to move our mission forward, *yet*. But if we create a list of the key policymakers passionate about our issue, then we can figure out who in our network might be able to introduce us.

You get the idea. Give it a try with whatever you believe your organization lacks the most and see what happens.

Adopting an abundance worldview can be a game changer. It is simply a choice to believe that there is more than enough for what you want to accomplish.

Once you believe that abundance is possible, the next step is to clarify what you want to accomplish so that you know how you will use the abundance you attract.

Articulate What You Want with a Theory of Change

A social change organization's activity is often determined by this fundamental scarcity-based question:

"How much can we accomplish with what we can raise?"

But if you truly believe that abundance—more than you could ever need—is possible, then the much better question to ask as a social change organization is:

"What do we want to accomplish?"

You answer this question by leading your board and staff to create your Theory of Change. A Theory of Change helps you articulate the social change you ultimately want to accomplish. It also does two crucial things that attract abundance: it aligns everyone inside the organization to a common vision and set of goals, and it convinces those outside the organization of the critical purpose of your work, compelling them to invest (their time, money, expertise, influence).

In essence, a Theory of Change *describes what you will use abundance to achieve.* It's a fundamental building block of attracting abundance, because it sets in motion a growing momentum that brings you more and more of what you need to accomplish the social change you seek.

That growing momentum looks like this:

- You articulate the social change your organization seeks to achieve (through a Theory of Change).

- Your board understands, is invested in, and is inspired by this future vision, so they give more time, energy, expertise, and money to the work.

- Your staff understands, is invested in, and is inspired by this future vision, which increases their energy, commitment, and productivity.

- You use this future vision to help funders, policymakers, partners, and influencers understand their critical role in it, inspiring them to invest, partner, and lend support (of all forms) in much bigger ways.

The very act of clearly articulating as a group what you want to accomplish builds momentum and energy that attracts increased dollars, people, and partners toward your social change goals.

Perhaps you are skeptical, so let me give you an example.

Several years ago Monique, the board chair of a statewide nonprofit that provides basic needs and social services throughout Texas, came to me. Her organization was losing money, staff was overworked, and she and her fellow board members were frustrated. They were providing too many services to too many people and lacked a clear, focused plan for achieving their mission. Understandably, their funders were confused and beginning to drift away. Their earned income efforts were losing money because staff members were spread too thinly over too many activities.

To address all these issues, I started by leading Monique, the rest of her board, and the staff to create a Theory of Change. The process of answering five key questions in the Theory of Change (we'll explore those shortly) forced the board and staff to have some hard conversations about where to focus, the social change they wanted to create, and what it would take to do that. We then used the Theory of Change to create a three-year strategic plan that had a strong focus on what the organization did well. As part of this planning process, board and staff made difficult decisions about cutting some programs that they were not qualified to effectively deliver, and they reinvested in the programs they could perform well. This increased clarity and focus allowed them to end financially draining programs while convincing more funders to invest in their stellar programs. Two years into their plan, they were raising substantially more money and creating a much more sustainable financial model, while (by the way) having a greater impact on the people they served.

The very act of clarifying what they wanted to accomplish was the catalyst that drove the organization to an abundance of money, people, and impact.

Create Your Theory of Change

You, too, can use this tool with your board and staff to reach similar clarity about what your organization wants to accomplish. The Theory of Change is based on five fundamental questions about your organization's work. Your answers to those five questions form the backbone of your organization's long-term goals, your strategy, and the work you need to do to get there.

Here are the five questions to create your Theory of Change.

1. Target population(s): what people do you seek to benefit or influence?

Your target population(s) are the specific individuals and/ or groups that you seek to change in order to move closer to achieving your organization's outcomes. In clarifying whom you are best positioned to benefit or influence, you will better direct your precious resources (staff, board, funders, volunteers) and become more likely to create the social change you seek.

If you run a social service nonprofit, your target population is probably your clients. If you lead an advocacy group, your target population is probably policymakers. If you direct a foundation, your target population includes your grantees and possibly policymakers, too. Often a social change organization has multiple target populations. For example, a school that works directly with both children and their parents would have both groups as separate target populations.

Your target populations do not include your funders. Although you would love to influence them to give you more money, their doing so will not by itself create social change; they are not your target population. Rather they are a means to enabling you to work with your target populations.

Your target populations are also not individuals or groups who could more effectively be served by other organizations. So investigate which other entities work with your target populations, to what effect, and how their efforts compare to those of your organization. Once you figure out who your competitors and collaborators are and where they shine, you can avoid target populations who are being better served by those other organizations.

Similarly, individuals or groups that you are not well positioned to help are not your target populations. Bighearted nonprofit leaders often add new client groups to their services, until these leaders realize that the organization is spread too thin to be effective. Although it may go against your nonprofit leader ethos, sometimes turning some people away to better serve others is the path toward greater social change.

2. External context: what are the relevant trends in or changes to your environment?

This is where your Theory of Change connects to the outside world. To achieve social change, you need to realize that your organization works within a complicated ecosystem of competitors and collaborators; demographic, economic, and cultural shifts; regulatory influences; and funding trends, among many other forces at play. And so, in this section of the Theory of Change, you articulate the external forces that currently, and potentially will, affect your target populations, your activities, and your outcomes.

Your work is part of a larger external environment, so resist the temptation to create your Theory of Change in a vacuum. Clearly articulate the relevant pieces of your external context and think about how these factors might help or hurt your efforts to achieve your desired outcomes.

3. Activities: how and where are your core competencies employed?

Your organization's core competencies are assets, expertise, or abilities your organization possesses that are unique and not easily replicable. Your organization does these better than anyone else.

The activities section of your Theory of Change describes how your organization will use its core competencies to achieve its desired outcomes. This is not a laundry list of all the various programs and initiatives you currently undertake, so resist the urge to create one. Rather, summarize the core work of your organization in a handful of bullet points (two to five). You may also need to make hard choices here, just as Monique's organization did in the social services nonprofit example I described above. If continuing a certain program no longer makes sense, because it doesn't fit with your core competencies or other organizations are better at providing those services, you may need to stop doing those activities.

You may also want to consider adding new activities. For example, a national nonprofit that has spent years working closely with the federal government might find itself, in recent years, blocked by a more conservative executive branch and a gridlocked Congress. In that case, the nonprofit might consider employing an alternative state-by-state approach where it works to change policy with individual states that are more receptive to its social change agenda. So, in looking at your core competencies and the external environment, it might make sense to craft a new set of activities for the social change you seek.

4. Outcomes: what changed conditions do you believe will result from these activities?

This is the most important section of your Theory of Change because it articulates the social change that your organization ultimately seeks to accomplish, both in the short term (one to three years or so) and the long term (five-plus years). You will hold yourselves accountable, both internally and externally, for accomplishing this change.

Understanding the difference between outputs and outcomes is important here. Outputs are items you have produced (number of students taught, number of teachers trained, number of museum visitors), but they do not speak to whether any social change has occurred. Outcomes, on the other hand, measure whether there has been any change in behaviors or attitudes (more students graduate from high school, more teachers use a more effective approach, more museum visitors see value in modern art).

Outcomes need to be measurable so that you know when and if you accomplish them. For example, an outcome such as "well-being is the new cultural norm" is not measurable because "well-being" could mean many different things to different people. Finding a tool that could measure a "cultural norm" could be tricky, so you will never know when or if your outcome has happened. But an outcome you could measure might be "the self-reported levels of happiness in our target populations increase by 30 percent."

In crafting your outcomes, be clear about what your organization can and cannot control. Social problems are complex, and no single organization or plan alone will completely solve them. Figure out what your organization can control and leave the rest to other organizations, the government, society at large, or the Universe.

5. Assumptions: what evidence suggests that this theory will result in change?

Your assumptions articulate why you have selected your particular model: the evidence that your activities will cause your desired outcomes.

Articulate these assumptions so that you can (1) analyze whether evidence supports the assumptions that are baked into your organization's approach—in other words, uncover why you do what you do, and analyze whether those reasons have merit; and (2) be transparent with your funders, partners, policymakers, and influencers about how confident you are in your approach.

CRAFTING YOUR organization's Theory of Change may take some time and involve some challenging conversations among board and staff. Keep in mind that your Theory of Change will evolve, too, and that these five areas are interdependent. As you get clarity in one section, you may need to change another—for example, if you revise your target populations, you may also need to shift your outcomes and/or your activities.

You will also want to test your assumptions, gather data, focus your target populations, perhaps abandon some well-loved activities, and figure out how you will measure your outcomes. But if you persevere, you will emerge with a clearer idea of what your organization exists to do and how you will do it.

Armed with a clear Theory of Change, you can then use it to revise your organization's vision and mission statements (which I discuss next), and craft your organization's strategic plan and corresponding financial model (which we'll discuss in the next chapter).

Your organization's vision and mission statements are critical to guiding your internal decisions and attracting external support. Both statements emanate from your Theory of Change, like this:

- **Vision.** Your vision statement articulates the social change you seek to achieve. It comes directly from the "outcomes" portion of your Theory of Change.

- **Mission.** Your mission statement describes the day-to-day work that you do, and with whom, to move toward that long-term vision. Your mission comes directly from the "target populations" and "activities" portions of your Theory of Change.

Creating a Theory of Change *before* you revise your vision and mission statements ensures that you come from a place of abundance when you craft these two fundamental statements that will guide your organization's work for years to come.

The very act of clarifying your ultimate destination, through a Theory of Change, will point you toward the abundance waiting for you.

Open Yourself (and Your Organization) to Receive

Once you know what you will accomplish with the abundance you seek, you can then open your organization to truly receive that abundance.

Seems bizarre, right? Nonprofits receive donations, time, supporters, and clients all the time. You could say that nonprofits are by definition great receivers. But nonprofit organizations often exist in an imbalanced and dysfunctional give-receive relationship. As I discussed in the previous chapter, nonprofit leaders are often over-givers, giving more than they receive, which has diminishing returns. To attract the abundance that your social change goals require, you want to build your organization's receiving muscle.

Gratitude is a powerful tool for attracting abundance, but only if it is true gratitude. And often in the nonprofit sector, gratitude is misapplied.

Have you ever said "thank you" to someone who didn't deserve your gratitude? For example:

- a board member who can't be bothered to show up, lift a finger, or perform in any significant way;

- a government-agency funder who demands more services for less investment on their part;

- a foundation leader who decides, seemingly out of nowhere, to commit their funding to a new, shiny object elsewhere;

- an unreliable, unproductive volunteer;

- a donor who drops worthless, in-kind items (outdated computers, broken furniture) on your nonprofit's doorstep.

None of these are gifts, and thus none of them warrants true gratitude. True gratitude is being thankful for receiving something that is of value to you. Let's be honest, a board member who deigns to be on your board but does very little to move the mission forward has little value to you. And a demanding, distracting, or frustrating funder is not valuable either. So why express gratitude for these things?

Instead, harness gratitude as the powerful tool that it is to bring more of what is valuable to your door. Distinguish between what is genuinely working (and thus what you are truly grateful for) and what isn't. If a funder offers unrestricted money or helpful advice and support, be truly grateful for her. If one or two board members shine, focus your gratitude on those people.

Because research shows that when you focus, through gratitude, on what is working, those things tend to grow.[9] And who doesn't need more helpful, effective, and tireless board members, funders, volunteers, and staff? Who doesn't need more money and time?

Start with this list to help you figure out what you are truly grateful for:

- Do particular board members leave their ego at the door and help however they can?

- Does a funder or two strongly believe in your mission and want to do everything in their power to help you achieve it?

- Are there volunteers who are tireless in their devotion and will do whatever you need, whenever you need it?

- Has a check randomly showed up at your door without any effort on your part?

- Do you see positive change happening for your clients or program participants?

- Do members of your staff go above and beyond to make your life easier?

Spend a few minutes every single day reviewing the top five truly valuable gifts (of time, care, support, connection, money) you and your organization received that day, and internally voice a heartfelt thank you for them. You could be grateful for something as simple as a board member who returned your phone call, the cleanliness of your office, or the delicious taste of your coffee this morning. These gifts don't have to be elaborate or massive. You just have to be truly grateful for them, whatever they are.

I encourage my clients to do this simple exercise of being grateful for five real gifts every day, and I do it myself before I go to bed every night. It is now my favorite part of the day, and I have found that the research demonstrating that gratitude makes what you are thankful for grow has been proven in my own life. The crazy thing is, limiting myself to five gifts is now a challenge. During the day, I often mentally note items to add to the list, which makes it far longer than five by bedtime. I promise you, gratitude is a magical tool that will open you to the abundance trying to reach you.

A second, and equally powerful, daily exercise that can further open you to receive is to establish your mindset for the day as soon as you wake in the morning. Before the endless to-do list or the feelings of inadequacy or the fear sets in, state an abundance intention for the day: "I intend to have an abundant day." When you first start doing this, you don't have to believe that you will see abundance. But set the intention and keep doing it. Pretty soon you will witness more and more abundance. What you focus on grows, remember?

These two simple, daily practices—of setting an abundance intention at the beginning of the day and expressing gratitude for five gifts at the end of the day—will dramatically open you and your organization to receiving more abundance.

One of my clients, Terrance, leads a community development nonprofit, and came to me particularly stuck in the muck of scarcity. He felt that the world reeked of lack. He lacked a capable board, enough staff, sufficient funding, a robust network... The list went on and on. I encouraged him to try these two practices—the daily abundance intention and gratitude list—for two weeks straight. At first, he was skeptical, but he was a good sport and gave it a try. He so enjoyed how he felt during those two weeks that he kept doing the two exercises. Two months later he received a $350,000 investment from a corporate donor he'd been cultivating for a year. Are the two related? I think so! Give it a try; see what happens.

Embrace the Less Than Perfect

Once you become an ace at being grateful for what is working, the next step in opening your organization to receive abundance is fully embracing what is not working.

My guess is that there is something you don't like about yourself as a leader and/or your organization. You might be the most successful, effective social change organization out there, but something makes you wary, ashamed, or embarrassed. Perhaps your program delivery model has some warts. Maybe you've never evaluated your programs, so you can't fully claim their successes. Perhaps you have an errant board member, an ineffective staff member, or a derelict website. Be brutally honest: what is limiting your organization and your mission? Whatever just jumped in your mind is worth exploring. Resist the temptation to tamp down that voice and to do what nonprofit leaders are so often told: "just make do with what you have." Instead, take a hard look at what isn't working and move toward compassionately fixing it. Because one of the ways we stop abundance from showing up on our doorstep is by blocking part of who and what we are.

This may be the most challenging thing I am asking you to do, because who among us wants to admit what we don't like about ourselves or our organizations? Here is where self-compassion is so critical. When you fully embrace your humanness, your imperfection, and your faults, you start to fully embrace all that you are. And when that happens, you begin to let in more abundance. Because if you are resisting part of who you are, or part of what your organization is, you are also resisting part of the abundance trying to reach you. When you defend yourself or your organization from what you don't want to admit, you also, unknowingly, protect yourself and your organization from what you desperately want and need.

Once you have fully acknowledged an imperfection, you can figure out, from a compassionate place, how to address it—whether to fix it or just laugh it off. If it isn't impeding your social change goals (like a typo or a meaningless mistake), fully let it go.

You can choose to see the limits in front of you, or the opportunities. And in seeing the opportunities—really, the abundance—you can accomplish so much more. History is full of examples of people who, contrary to their contemporaries, believed that scarcity could be overcome. People who believed that something beyond the current perceived limits was possible. The combustion engine, air travel, the polio vaccine, refrigeration all started with someone, somewhere, believing that scarcity could be overcome.

Your belief in abundance sets your organization, your board, your staff, your funders, and ultimately your social change goals on a path toward what you may have once thought was impossible. In embracing an abundance mindset, you lead the way to a more sustainable and effective future for your organization and, more importantly, for the social change you seek. Embracing an abundance mindset is the critical first step to allowing in all that money that you badly need. So, now let's talk about how you make money your new best friend.

Make Money Your New Best Friend

"What we really want to do is what we are really meant to do. When we do what we are meant to do, money comes to us, doors open for us, we feel useful, and the work we do feels like play to us."

JULIA CAMERON

ERE'S THE BRUTAL truth: the way that money flows to social change efforts is horribly broken. For the most part, nonprofit leaders fundraise for scraps, are beholden to demanding and often distracting funders, deliver services at a loss, and chase ill-suited business ideas for earned income. Nonprofit organizations are typically hobbled by outdated technology, ineffective systems, and insufficient staffing. And nonprofit leaders often feel guilty about, or unworthy of, asking for the money they truly need to realize their social change goals.

If we are truly serious about creating real change to social problems, it is going to take lots and lots (and lots) of money. These are complex, deeply ingrained problems we are looking to solve. Whether the problem is homelessness, hunger, inequitable education, poverty, or crumbling democracy, real solutions require so much more than a Band-Aid. I'm not telling you anything you don't already know—you cannot fundamentally change broken systems on a shoestring budget. But we have forever been telling nonprofit leaders, and you have been telling yourselves, that a shoestring is all you get.

That's messed up.

So, the first step in attracting the kind of money your solution requires is to admit that you need much more money than you probably currently have. Because you have no hope of getting what you can't even admit to yourself (let alone your board and funders) that you need.

I want to point out that although the majority of this book applies to all social change organizations, this chapter on money is focused on the nonprofit business model (as opposed to foundation or corporate social responsiblity business models, which could be the subjects of whole other books themselves). But if you are a foundation leader, a government decision-maker, or a director of corporate social responsibility dollars this chapter still applies to you. The very fact that you direct funds means that you are a key player in changing how money flows to social change initiatives. It is imperative that you understand how money can be put to work to create effective social change.

Money Can Be Lovable

"Money" is such a dirty word in the social change sector. Let's be honest, it's a dirty word in Western society. We covet money, we obsesses about it, we desire it, but we also feel guilty about desiring it; we fear that it will corrupt. It's an exhausting love-hate relationship.

We see all around us the greed of bad actors with extractive policies that result in wealth inequality. There are countless examples where money has been used to exclude or harm. But money is not the culprit. Money is simply a tool, and like any other tool it can be used for good or ill. So what we really need is more people like you who are creating social value—something additive to your community, your city, your country, our planet—by directing more money toward social good.

To do that, you must learn to love—I mean *adore*—money. Eschew the typical nonprofit relationship to money, which is to resist it—by fearing it, angsting about it, getting frustrated with it, or ignoring it altogether. Instead, get cozy with this powerful social change tool.

Money is simply a shorthand for the exchange of goods and services. We may have long ago moved from the barter system to the currency system, but the underlying concept is the same—money represents an exchange of items for value. So, if you are truly creating social value, then money will flow to you.

That is, if you don't get in its way.

Stop Resisting Money

Social changemakers—from nonprofit CEOs to board members to program officers to foundation heads and beyond—typically oppose the flow of money that seeks to find value. By "resist," I mean the act of defending yourself or your organization from money. Why in the world would any social change leader want to defend their organization from money, that most coveted of resources?

Here are some ways, consciously or not, that you may be resisting money.

Thinking there is not enough money

So often nonprofit leaders (and, weirdly, funders, who have lots of it) think of money as a scarce resource. But money is everywhere. As I mentioned before, wealth is growing, and there are billionaires desperate to give away their money but unable to do so. Instead they are attracting more money and growing their wealth. So, there is a lot of money; it is just not reaching your organization in the way you need it to. That's a problem, but a fixable one. Stop resisting money by thinking there isn't enough of it.

Working to keep costs as low as possible

Most nonprofits subsist—maintaining their work at a minimal level—because the goal is to keep any and all costs as low as humanly possible. But this constantly striving to pinch pennies comes at a great loss. My first nonprofit boss and lifelong mentor was the executive director of the Oregon Children's Foundation, a statewide childhood literacy nonprofit. Mary was skilled at getting things for free or very cheap. The ultimate reward, in her mind, was more money for her nonprofit. But in her eternal quest for a bargain, she was wasting her valuable time. An hour of her time spent negotiating with the printer manufacturer to get a $100 discount was an hour she could have spent calling a potential major donor or encouraging a board member to do more for the organization. I love Mary dearly, but her desire to keep costs as low as possible meant that she was greatly devaluing her organization's top asset (her time as the leader), and putting herself and her organization in a place of scarcity.

Worrying that money could reduce your organization's virtue

Probably stemming from the historical charity mindset discussed in chapter one, in our society, poverty equals virtue, especially when it comes to nonprofits. Some social change leaders unwittingly keep their organizations poor by thinking an influx of money would somehow compromise their value and their good work. This is another form of gaslighting and placing unfair standards on the social change sector. We don't fault Amazon, Facebook, Google, or Apple for being rich. We think they are the most innovative, value-producing entities in the world. If you want to do more than good work, if you want to do something really big—like, I don't know, change the world—you are going to have to be rich, really rich, as an organization. But if you think that being a poor organization holds virtue, then you are essentially telling money to take a hike.

THESE AND other resistant thoughts about money serve only to keep you, your staff, your board, and even your funders locked in opposition to all the money that seriously wants to reach you. But there is hope. If you can change how you understand, create strategy around, ask for, and use money, you can fundamentally transform how money reaches your work. When you embrace money as a helpful, joyful tool for achieving social change, suddenly the floodgates open.

How Money Flows to Nonprofits

Let's start by understanding how money works in the social change sector. There are three main categories of revenue in the sector:

- Earned income is the sale of goods and services, like the patient fees at a nonprofit hospital, student tuition at nonprofit universities, museum ticket sales, licensing, advertising, and cause-related marketing.

- Government contracts include local, regional, state, and federal funding that can come in the form of fees-for-service or grants.

- Philanthropic donations are from foundations, corporations, and individuals.

The way these various revenue streams flow to the American nonprofit sector has looked largely the same for the past several decades, as illustrated in the graphic that follows.

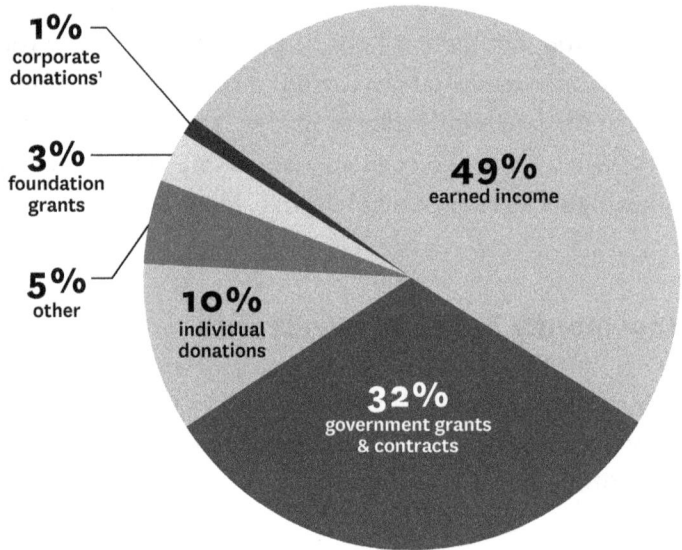

1%
corporate donations[1]

3%
foundation grants

5%
other

10%
individual donations

49%
earned income

32%
government grants & contracts

A big misconception in the social change sector is that philanthropy, and in particular foundation grants, are a significant portion of all the money flowing to nonprofits. But you can see that philanthropy (individual donations, foundation grants, and corporate donations) makes up only 14 percent of all revenue in the sector, and foundation grants make up only 3 percent. Philanthropy overall, and foundation funding in particular, cannot possibly fund the social change sector at a significant level.

It is also important to understand *both* of the two different kinds of money that can flow to a nonprofit:

- Revenue is the day-to-day, ongoing money required to run programs and an organization. At a shelter, for example, revenue buys meals, beds, sheets, job-training programs, and staff time.

- Capital is the one-time infusion of money that builds or grows an organization. In the homeless shelter example, capital purchases a better system for gathering data on clients, a donor database, a program evaluation, the first year or two of a development director's salary and/or other revenue-generating staff.

Historically, most nonprofit leaders have worked to attract only revenue, because they thought any money that didn't go to a program—like *capital*—was taboo. This lack of organization-building capital has resulted in anemic nonprofit organizations that have little hope of becoming social change powerhouses.

As I have mentioned, for-profit companies enjoy many advantages over nonprofits, one of which is that they have more access to capital. Another advantage is that for-profits typically have only one customer type, whereas nonprofits have at least two. It breaks down like this: Customers of a business usually both *benefit from* and *pay for* the products or services they receive from a business. Whereas the customers of nonprofits typically include:

- those who *benefit from* a nonprofit's products or services (clients), and

- those who *pay for* the nonprofit's products or services (philanthropic or government funders).

Sometimes a nonprofit will have earned income streams, as mentioned above, but even then, those earned revenues never cover all the costs of the nonprofit or its programs. If they did, the organization would be a for-profit business. Therefore, by definition, a nonprofit's products and services are never fully funded by the people who benefit from those products or services.

Perhaps because nonprofits have two types of customers, the prices of products and services in the nonprofit sector for the most part have been kept artificially and detrimentally low. As we discussed in the previous chapter, the "starvation cycle" emerged when funders (the second of a nonprofit's two customer groups) tried to keep the prices they would pay for a nonprofit's services as low as possible.

One concept from the business world has somehow not made its way to the nonprofit sector: "Price signals value." The idea is that, for example, the higher price of a $25 bottle of wine versus a $10 bottle of wine signals to the consumer that the more expensive wine has much greater value than the less expensive one. But the various components that go into manufacturing the wine likely cost roughly the same amount. So, the two wines are not inherently different (apologies to all of the wine connoisseurs out there); we, as a society, just choose to value the two wines differently, because the wine producer signals this to us in how they price their wine.

In the nonprofit sector the goal is to constantly keep the price of the services that funders purchase as low as possible. And if you, as a nonprofit leader, choose to do this, you signal to your funders, your clients, your board, your staff, and yourself that what you create is low in value. I'm not suggesting that this is intentional; it is subconscious, but it's still a problem. And as we have been discussing throughout this book, it is madness that we don't sufficiently recognize the tremendous social value that social change leaders create.

So the challenge then—or, really, the opportunity—is to price your social change in a way that signals its tremendous value. Instead of telling your funders that the cost of delivering your services is as low as you can possibly get it, educate them about the tremendous value of the services you deliver. Then demand (in a nice way!) that your funders pay what it truly costs to deliver those high-quality services. In embracing the true cost of the social value you create, you will begin to attract the money you need to create the social change you seek. You do that by moving from the back-breaking work of struggling to make financial ends meet to creating a sustainable financial model for your endeavors.

What Is a Sustainable Nonprofit?

"Sustainable nonprofit" sounds sexy, right? Well, yeah, I think so! But you might disagree. Certainly it is the Holy Grail of the nonprofit sector. Everyone wants it, but few achieve it. So, what is it? Let's start by understanding what nonprofit sustainability is *not*.

Nonprofit sustainability is NOT earned income

Moving away from a reliance on private philanthropy and becoming "self-sufficient" through earned income sources (the sale of goods or services) is not sustainability. Relying on a business model of mostly earned income is rarely possible for nonprofits. They are often born out of an imbalance (income inequality, racial inequity, failing education systems, and so on) created by the market economy. So, rarely can a nonprofit figure out how to make the market pay to fix a problem that it created in the first place. The vast majority of nonprofits will never be fully self-sustaining through earned income. In other words, your nonprofit will likely always need to be subsidized by non-earned sources like philanthropy and government grants.

Nonprofit sustainability is NOT multiyear, unrestricted funding

Although more multiyear, unrestricted dollars flowing to nonprofits would be a positive step, foundations are largely the only nonprofit funding source able or willing to make unrestricted, multiyear commitments. Government funding is never unrestricted, and individuals rarely make multiyear commitments. And even if all foundation funders made these commitments, as we discussed above, foundation funding only ever totals 3 percent of all the revenue flowing to the nonprofit sector. So more foundations giving more unrestricted gifts would simply not be significant enough to achieve nonprofit sustainability.

Nonprofit sustainability is NOT full-cost funding

In recent years, some in the social change sector have pushed for funder understanding and funding a nonprofit's full costs (both the direct and indirect costs). Although this is absolutely a part of nonprofit sustainability, I don't think funding full costs tells the whole story of what the long-term sustainability of a nonprofit looks like.

NONE OF these definitions of "nonprofit sustainability" works. They are too narrow, too unrealistic, or inaccurate.

In my mind, nonprofit sustainability happens when nonprofits attract and effectively use enough and the right kinds of money necessary to achieve their long-term outcome goals.

Let's break that down, starting with what nonprofits want to accomplish, and work backward from there:

"... to achieve their long-term outcome goals."

To create a sustainable nonprofit, you must articulate what you are ultimately trying to achieve. As we discussed in chapter three, you cannot hope to attract enough money to create the change you seek if you don't first know what that is. A Theory of Change helps your board and staff articulate these long-term outcome goals.

Sustainability happens when nonprofits attract and effectively use enough and the right kinds of money necessary to achieve their long-term outcome goals.

"... effectively use ... money"

Articulating your desired long-term outcomes is not enough. You must then determine what staff, board, volunteers, systems, technology, marketing, and other resources you need to get there. You want to articulate the business model you will employ—and the corresponding money required—to realize your long-term outcome goals (how you will "effectively use money"). And I don't mean the bare-bones version. I mean what it will really cost to achieve the long-term outcomes you seek. The Bridgespan Group created a very useful tool for calculating the full costs of your nonprofit's business model.[2]

"... attract ... enough and the right kinds of money"

Figuring out what your outcome goals are going to cost is not enough. You also have to crack the other side of the money equation, which is how to bring that money in the door. A smart financial strategy attracts money that is the right fit for your organization. Be strategic (not reactive) about how money flows to your organization (philanthropy, government grants, earned income). It might be that you focus solely on private sources, or you may have a mix of government and earned sources. But the ways in which you bring money in must align with your core competencies and your mission.

ULTIMATELY, NONPROFIT sustainability means that both *the way money comes in your door* and *the way money goes out your door* happen in a smart, strategic, abundant way that achieves the social change you seek.

Nonprofit sustainability, then, is a critical shift away from the narrow and dysfunctional *fundraising* approach that the vast majority of nonprofits employ, to a more robust and sustainable social change *financing* approach.

Move from *Nonprofit Fundraising* to *Social Change Financing*

If you truly want to create social change, you have to break out of the narrow view that traditional *fundraising* will bring you enough of the money you need. Instead you want to work to secure the *financing* necessary to achieve the social change you seek.

Often nonprofit fundraising is a lot of "shiny object syndrome." Boards and staffs so abhor fundraising that they desperately search for a magic bullet to make it all go away. Sometimes that magic bullet is an endowment, sometimes it's earned income—more recently it has been crowdfunding, giving days, or the latest social media challenge. But the problem with shiny object syndrome is that it seeks only a one-time infusion of money. A single windfall is not a sustainable business model.

A sustainable business model means consistent, reliable streams of revenue and, when you need it, capital flowing to your organization regularly, and fairly predictably.

Moving from fundraising to financing is a fundamental pivot from the scarcity approach of just trying to scrape by within the perceived limits to an abundance mindset of knowing whatever you truly want to create is possible. So instead of asking the *scarcity* question:

"How much money can we raise?"

Ask the *abundance* question:

"How much money will it take to
accomplish our goals?"

With the abundance question, you are limited only by what you set out to accomplish, not by the money available, because, as we have learned, *more than enough money is available.*

Let's further break down the difference between nonprofit fundraising and social change financing. The chart on the following page shows how the two approaches differ. See which column your organization falls into most often:

THE NONPROFIT FUNDRAISING APPROACH	THE SOCIAL CHANGE FINANCING APPROACH
Money is a source of constant worry and anxiety.	Money is embraced as an effective, productive avenue to achieving social change.
Board and staff are exhausted, burned-out.	Board and staff are energized, excited.
The organization's money-raising function is split between multiple people, and/or siloed from the rest of the organization.	All staff who work to raise money are fully integrated with one another and with the other areas of the organization.
A few board members help bring money in the door.	Every board member has a specific and well-understood role in the organization's money engine.
The organization's revenue mix is unpredictable and unreliable.	The organization has a robust, fairly predictable year-over-year revenue mix.
The organization's money-raising activities typically cost more than they return.	All/most of the organization's money-raising activities have a high return on investment.
The organization's money-raising infrastructure (technology, marketing, systems) are inefficient, ineffective, outdated.	The organization has high-quality, efficient money-raising infrastructure.

As you can see (and you may currently be experiencing), nonprofit fundraising is exhausting, demoralizing, anxiety-ridden, confusing, unpredictable, and outdated. Social change financing, on the other hand, is productive, energizing, integrated, well understood, robust, predictable, efficient—abundant. Which sounds better?

Social change financing
is productive, energizing,
integrated, well under-
stood, robust, predictable,
efficient—abundant.

Align Money with Your Mission

In a fundraising approach, you typically think about money on one side of your organization, and everything else the organization does on the other. To embrace a social change financing approach, you need to fully integrate money into everything your organization does. You do this by aligning money with your mission and core competencies. In a sustainable nonprofit organization, your mission, your core competencies, and your financial model exist in alignment:

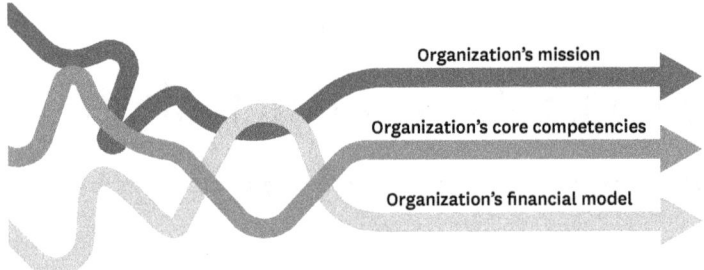

Organization's mission

Organization's core competencies

Organization's financial model

In alignment, your nonprofit's mission is supported by your organization's core competencies (what you do better than anyone else), which both line up with how you attract and use money.[3] In other words, your financial model complements, rather than detracts from, your nonprofit's mission and most effective work.

But when one or two of these three elements are misaligned, chaos ensues. Here are some examples:

- An organization generates money and operates great programs, but can't bring it all together into a coherent single purpose. This is otherwise known as "mission creep."

- An organization's leadership clearly knows what they want to accomplish (mission) and can raise money for it, but don't have the right competencies to execute. They don't have the right expertise on staff, are unable to deliver programs, or can't access the right influencers.

- An organization has a defined mission and achieves results, but cannot raise enough money to keep it all going—the staff lacks financial expertise, chases the wrong types of revenue, and spins its wheels with inefficient fundraising activities.

- An organization has a compelling mission but lacks both an effective way to operate and a sustainable revenue stream.

Whether one of these sounds like your organization, I think you'll agree that none of these scenarios will result in lasting social change. If you want to be successful at achieving that, you need to fully align mission, money, and competency.

Tie Financial Strategy to Your Organizational Strategy

Once you have figured out your mission/money alignment (or misalignment), you want to create a strategy for attracting enough, and the right kinds of money to deliver on your long-term outcomes.

Your nonprofit's strategic plan is really just a short-term view of your Theory of Change. While your Theory of Change charts what your organization ultimately wants to accomplish over the next ten, twenty, fifty years—however long your desired outcomes might take—your strategic plan charts your more immediate path toward those outcomes. Typically a strategic plan lays out the next three to five years of your organization's future. It is as if you are attempting to drive from Toronto to Mexico City. You need to know that Mexico City is your final destination before you can figure out which direction to start driving. Once you know that, then you can plan which road you will take, and determine that Detroit will likely be your first stopping point.

As part of charting the next three to five years of your organization's work, you want to create a corresponding financial model that articulates how much that work will cost, its time frame, and what revenue and capital you will raise to exceed those costs. So, with your strategic plan in hand, you can then ask:

"How much money, over what time frame, do we need to achieve the goals of our strategic plan?"

Because if you truly want to bring your strategic plan to fruition, you must connect it to the money it will take to execute it.

You do that in three steps.

1. Determine your expenses for each goal

Review each goal of your strategic plan and figure out what it will *actually* cost (in current and new staff, contractors, technology, meetings, marketing, supplies, travel, and so on) to make it happen.

2. Attach those expenses to a time frame

Project those expenses over the time frame of your strategic plan. If you have a three-year strategic plan, determine what your organization's expenses must be each year for the next three years to achieve the goals of your strategic plan. Resist the strong temptation to simply project your current expenses plus a slight increase for inflation over the next three years. Factor in what it will truly take to effectively deliver on your strategic plan. Move from the Band-Aid budget you have likely always relied on and instead create a bold projection (enough talented staff, state-of-the-art technology) for what you need to knock it out of the park.

3. Project your revenue to exceed your expenses

Then plot out how much revenue (and maybe capital, too, if it makes sense for your organization) you need, and from which revenue sources, to exceed those expenses. Yes, I said "exceed" because, as we learned in chapter one, healthy nonprofits, just like healthy businesses, need robust reserve funds to be flexible, innovative, and strategic.

As you project your revenue, keep in mind that there are many ways you can raise money, so only include profitable money-raising activities that align with your mission and core competencies. How can you figure out which are most profitable?

Calculate Your Cost to Raise a Dollar

Staffs and/or boards typically have a limited amount of time to spend on raising money. So when crafting your financing plan, you need to make sure that those limited resources raise as much money as possible. That means you must analyze which of the money-raising activities your nonprofit employs are the most profitable.

You do this by calculating the "cost to raise a dollar" of each way that you bring money in the door (events, individual solicitations, government contracts, foundation grants, earned income, and so on).

Calculating the cost to raise a dollar of a money-raising activity has two steps.

1. Calculate net revenue

Gross revenue is the total of all the money an activity brought in your door. Often, nonprofit leaders focus on this figure to determine if an activity—say, a fundraising gala—was successful. But looking at gross revenue for a gala, for example, is inaccurate, because you don't keep all that revenue. Some money goes out the door to pay for the gala. These costs are both *direct* (the band, venue, food, invitations, and staff that worked directly on the activity) and *indirect* (the board's and executive director's time spent on the gala). You only really know how much money you made once you subtract the costs that went in to the gala. So, your first step is to calculate the net revenue of a money-raising activity:

net revenue = gross revenue – fundraising costs (direct and indirect)

Let's pretend that a nonprofit organization with a $2 million annual budget throws an annual gala with a band, catering, and an auction. One staff member spends half their time organizing the event, and a board committee helps sell tables and provides oversight. Most of the board and staff also help set up and attend the gala. At the end of the evening the organization brings in *gross* revenue of $300,000. They should be thrilled that they made 15 percent of their annual budget in one night, right?

Wrong.

The gross revenue of $300,000 tells only part of the story. It ignores the direct and indirect costs of the event. Let's say that *total costs* of the gala were:

$100,000 (band, food, venue, and so on) + $75,000 (the dollar value of staff and board member time) = $175,000

Therefore, the net revenue of this event is:

$300,000 (gross revenue) - $175,000 (direct and indirect costs) = $125,000 net revenue

2. Determine cost to raise a dollar

Now we can determine how much it cost this nonprofit to generate a net revenue of $125,000, with this formula:

$$\text{cost to raise a dollar} = \frac{\textbf{total costs (direct and indirect)}}{\textbf{net revenue}}$$

So, in our gala example, the cost to raise a dollar would look like this:

$$\frac{\$175,000}{\$125,000} = \$1.40 \text{ cost to raise a dollar}$$

Putting on this gala cost the organization $1.40 for each dollar raised—in other words, it cost more money to hold the event than the event raised. That's not an attractive return, is it? Although this organization did make money, the cost of making that money was far larger than the money they made.

Often when I share a calculation like this with nonprofit leaders, they become defensive. "But what about the intangible benefits to an event, like its ability to raise awareness?" If you feel some of your money-raising activities have intangible marketing or community-building benefits, that's great. But if those are the only benefits, and you didn't make more than you spent, it was not a money-raising event. So, be clear on what you are trying to accomplish with everything you do and then determine if you actually achieve that end result. If it costs you $175,000 to make $125,000, that was not a money-raising event. Once you know that, you can determine if you want to continue to spend that money for the other intangible benefits it may produce.

You can use these two calculations to understand how effective your money-making activities actually are. You can then compare activities and see which have the lowest cost to raise a dollar. And even better, you can then direct investments of money and time away from costly activities and into more profitable ones.

The Catalyst That Is Capacity Capital

To be as profitable as possible in your money-raising activities you may need to invest in your money-raising infrastructure—the staff, technology, and systems you employ to bring in money. Remember that an investment in your money-raising infrastructure is an investment in your mission—there is no mission without money.

Often the act of smartly investing in money-raising strategies and functions can dramatically shift how money flows to your social change effort. You do this through something called capacity capital.

Believe me when I say that capacity capital will make the difference between the anemic nonprofits of today and the social change powerhouses of tomorrow. Capacity capital (also referred to in the sector as "growth capital," "growth equity," or "philanthropic equity") is an incredibly powerful, but little-understood and rarely used, form of money that can strengthen and grow your organization, particularly its money-raising function. It can be a game-changer.

My guess is that your nonprofit, like so many of your peer organizations, lacks enough staff, systems, space, support, and training to maintain your current operations, let alone grow in a sustainable way. In other words, you don't have enough people and systems to allow your brilliant social change efforts to spread far and wide.

You may lack some (if not all) of these things:

- highly skilled fundraising staff;

- efficient and effective technology to track your clients, funders, advocates, volunteers, supporters, and influencers;

- compelling marketing strategies and materials (website, emails, print efforts, messaging) to attract your key audiences;

- program evaluations and performance management systems to demonstrate the social value you create, strengthen your programs, and attract larger investments;

- High-quality, ongoing professional development, training, and coaching opportunities for your staff;

- long-term planning and strategy;

- effective donor and prospect research.

These are all areas where nonprofit leaders—who have been operating for so long under the broken social change sector—cut corners. But these factors make an organization strong, and that makes the difference between creating sustainable social change and not.

Capacity capital is a one-time infusion of a significant amount of money from a handful of your closest donors and/or board members. The amount of capital could range from $50,000 for a new software package to track donors to multimillion dollars over three years to fund new money-raising staff, database systems, and marketing. The amount of capacity capital you might raise depends on what organization-building elements your organization needs and whether you can compel your close donors and/or board members to invest.

You have no hope of growing your financial model if you keep doing the same things, with the same people, and the same tools. So, if you want a significant change in your ability to bring money in the door, you likely need to invest in your revenue-generating function on the front end. That's where capacity capital comes in.

Long before I launched Social Velocity, I led the marketing and development department at KLRU, Austin's PBS station. When I started there we struggled to retain current donors and attract new ones because we didn't have enough and the right staff, technology, and systems. Capacity capital was the answer. We raised a total of $350,000 in capacity capital from six close donors. We used this one-time influx of money to add key revenue-generating staff, purchase a new donor database and online giving software, conduct market research on our donors and prospects, revamp our marketing, and train staff. After two years, our annual revenue grew by $1.6 million (a 40 percent increase), and the number of donors grew by 36 percent to over 19,000. The relatively small investment of capacity capital from a handful of our donors elevated our money-raising function to a whole new playing field.

Capacity capital, if right for your nonprofit, could grow your organization's staff and systems so that you can attract more funders and supporters—all things that can help you get that much closer to your social change vision.

But what if you don't know what capacity your organization lacks? I get it. Your organization, like so many nonprofits, may have spent so many years in scarcity that you have no idea what is holding it back and where you can invest in capacity-building efforts. If this is the case for you, the first step is to do an organizational assessment to uncover what is limiting the organization and where you could invest in organization building. I and other consultants can conduct such an assessment, or you can choose to do an organizational self-assessment.[4]

Typically, an organizational assessment analyzes the capacity of seven key areas. So, as a beginning exercise, ask yourself these questions to determine which area(s) likely lack capacity in your organization:

- **Strategy.** Does your nonprofit have a long-term strategy that integrates money, programs, and operations? Does your strategy help articulate the value your nonprofit provides in order to compel outsiders to invest?

- **Mission and vision.** Does your nonprofit have clear, compelling vision and mission statements? Does your vision boldly describe the social change you seek? Does your mission articulate the daily work toward that vision?

- **Program delivery and impact.** Is your nonprofit strategic about which programs to grow and which to cut? Do you measure the effect of your programs on clients? Are your programs financially viable, or are too many of your programs mission rich but cash poor? Are the systems and technology you use to deliver your programs the best they can be?

- **Board and staff leadership.** Is your board engaged and invested? Are board members actively connecting the organization to people, resources, and partnerships? Does your staff have the knowledge, talent, and experience necessary? And are they structured and managed effectively?

- **Financial model.** Does your funding mix fit well with your mission and core competencies? Are there new revenue streams to pursue? Are any fundraising activities costly rather than profitable? Are the staff, technology, and systems used to raise money the best they can be?

- **External partnerships.** Do you have enough high-quality external relationships to execute your strategy? Are you constantly working to strengthen or grow the right partnerships in the right ways?

- **Marketing and communications.** Do you make a compelling case for your work and why outsiders should support it? Once you've made the case, are you using the right marketing channels (website, social media, events, email) to attract your target funders, volunteers, and advocates?

Wherever you've answered "no" or "not really" is likely an area where you could invest in your organizational capacity. Start brainstorming what investments you could make in each area where your organizational capacity is limited. For example, if you don't have a compelling, actionable long-term strategy, you could invest in a robust strategic planning process. If you don't measure the effect of your programs on your clients, you could invest in a program evaluation. Once you create your list of capacity investments, you can then research the cost of each, add all those costs together, and determine exactly how much capacity capital you require.

Cultivate a Culture of Money and Mission

Beyond investing in a strong organization, shifting the culture of your board, staff, and funders is also critical to achieving financial sustainability.

In recent years there has been much talk about creating a "culture of philanthropy" in nonprofit organizations. In their report *Beyond Fundraising*, the Evelyn and Walter Haas, Jr. Fund defined a culture of philanthropy as a situation where everyone within an organization values fundraising "as a mission-aligned program of the organization."[5]

That is great, but I don't think it takes the definition far enough. Rather, to create social change financing, you want to create a "culture of money and mission" among your board, staff, and funders. This culture of money and mission becomes the compelling force that attracts the amount of money you need to achieve your social change goals.

Here are the key elements present in a social change organization that has a robust culture of money and mission. See which ones apply to your organization:

- The staff and board make any decisions about programs (for example, whether to add, cut, or change program delivery methods) by first understanding the financial implications of those decisions.

- The staff pursues only revenue-generating activities that clearly fit with the organization's core competencies and mission.

- The board analyzes and offers guidance about the financial position of the organization (how money comes in and how it goes out) at every board meeting.

- A single staff member (or an integrated team of staff) is responsible for planning and managing all revenue lines (this might be the executive director in a small nonprofit, or the development director/chief revenue officer and her team in a large organization).

- Every single board member contributes to the financial model (by making a personal contribution, securing a contribution from their company or foundation, and/or actively fundraising or raising earned income from others).

- The program team and money-raising team constantly work together to determine how to fund programs.

- The board members and executive director work often and closely with the head staff money raiser (for example, the development director or chief revenue officer) to help raise money.

- There is a long-term financial strategy that all staff and the board understand and have confidence in.

If the majority of these apply to your organization, congratulations! You are definitely in the minority in the social change sector, and good for you!

If few or none of these apply to your organization, take comfort in the fact that you are far from alone. Few social change organizations enjoy a robust culture of money and mission.

But the good news is that you have the power to change. By helping your board and staff—and even your funders!—embrace money as an incredibly useful tool for achieving your social change goals, money can become an abundant resource for you.

Here's how to shift yourself, your board, staff, and funders to an abundant money mindset.

Make Each Board Member Key to Your Financial Engine

Probably the most controversial factor in the culture of money and mission elements above is the idea that every single board member should contribute to their nonprofit's financial model. I have seen this idea strike fear in the hearts of nonprofit leaders when I have shared it.

But there are several reasons why compelling every single board member to contribute to your financial model is a no-brainer. First, the board of directors must be a nonprofit's staunchest supporters, most vocal advocates, and most committed allies. If you can't depend on your board to work tirelessly to ensure not only the achievement of your mission but also financial sustainability, you can't possibly expect those outside your organization to care, let alone invest. Second, if some are allowed to be board members in name only and not required to have any skin in the game, then it becomes very difficult to compel another board member to significantly invest their time and resources. Third, if there is no bar that must cleared to become a board member, then nothing separates a board member from just an interested member of the public. Finally, when you allow an individual board member to have a say in programmatic and organizational decisions without fully understanding and contributing to your financial model, you create an enormous disconnect between mission and money.

So, yes, I believe each board member should somehow contribute to the financial model of the nonprofit they serve. Being a member of a board must come with some level of commitment, both of time and of money-raising effort.

But fear not, making each board member contribute to your financial model doesn't have to be as scary as you might imagine. I define "contribute" very broadly—it can take many forms (and some don't even include the exchange of money).

A board member could contribute to your financial model by:

- telling a potential donor why he believes so strongly in your nonprofit's mission;

- connecting a peer foundation or corporate decision-maker to your nonprofit;

- serving as a business advisor to your nonprofit's earned income venture;

- making thank-you phone calls or writing thank-you notes to your nonprofit's largest donors;

- hosting a "friend-raiser" at their home to evangelize your nonprofit and its work;

- and, of course, writing a check for any amount (no matter how small).

This list is just a start. All these (relatively simple) activities move your nonprofit's ability to attract money forward. Make contributing to your nonprofit's financial model a clear expectation of each board member, every year that they serve, and I promise you won't regret it.

Staff Your Financial Model Like You Mean It

Once your entire board is contributing to your financial model, look at how you staff that financial model.

The nonprofit sector is currently experiencing a crisis in recruiting and retaining top fundraising talent. A report by CompassPoint titled *UnderDeveloped* uncovered that many nonprofit development directors are unhappy and are about to leave their positions or be fired, and many executive directors are unable to find well-qualified fundraisers.[6]

There are likely many reasons for this staffing crisis, but chief among them, in my mind, is that nonprofit leaders rarely think of their lead money person in a holistic, empowered way. To truly use money as a tool, stop thinking about your money-raising functions in small, siloed ways. Analyze your entire financial model and hire someone who can develop and execute a strategy for strengthening and growing *all* aspects of that financial model. If, for example, you manage government grants, run an earned income enterprise, and fundraise from philanthropists, hire someone who can understand, create, and execute a strategy for all those revenue streams.

To do that, you also need to pay enough to attract top money-raising talent. A common refrain in the nonprofit sector is "we don't have enough money to pay for a top fundraiser." It seems like a catch-22, but remember that capacity capital can provide a way out. If you don't have the current budget to pay a market rate for the type of money-raiser your social change goals require, raise capacity capital to fund the first two years of the position. A year or two into a talented money-raiser's tenure, she will be raising her own salary many times over while growing your overall financial model. But don't forget to raise enough capacity capital to buy her the money-raising systems (and potentially additional staff) that she might need, as well.

Once you have a talented money-raiser on board, empower her to develop and execute an overall financial strategy tied to your strategic plan, as we discussed earlier in this chapter. But don't faultily assume, as many nonprofit leaders do, that your new fundraiser will execute that financial strategy all by herself. If you are going to align mission and money, make sure that *everyone* in your organization (board and staff) understands their role in bringing money in the door. That means every board member plays a role in the financial model, and every staff member—even those who don't have dollar goals in their job description—understands that they can (and will) play a role in creating a sustainable organization. That might mean talking to prospects and donors, giving program tours, or writing thank-you notes, to name a few examples.

At the end of the day, your chief money-raiser's ultimate role is to marshal the entire board and staff to execute your organization's long-term financial strategy. That's the path not just to financial sustainability but to abundance!

Make Your Funders Your Equal

Now we turn to funders. I could write a whole book about the dysfunctions that exist between funders and those who are funded. It won't come as a shock to you that there is a troubling power imbalance between those who hold the purse strings and those who don't. Indeed, many books have been written recently about how philanthropy in particular is serving only to perpetuate inequity.[7] A fundamental change is necessary among funders, to be sure.

But as I said in the Introduction, I believe that change starts with the individual. So, although nonprofit leaders currently carry a heavy burden where funding and funders are concerned, change will come when individual nonprofit leaders start demanding a different relationship with their funders.

To truly make money your new best friend you have to fundamentally shift how you think about, work with, and talk to your funders. Whether your "funders" are foundation program officers, individual donors, earned income customers, corporate managers, government agency decision-makers, or some combination of all these, you have the power to fundamentally shift what is likely a dysfunctional relationship.

If you are like the majority of social change leaders, you believe (consciously or not) that those who have money (funders) are inherently better than those who ask for that money (nonprofit leaders).

But that is categorically untrue. To accomplish your social change work, you need the money that a potential funder controls. In the social change sector we often ignore that a funder also—and just as importantly—needs you to do the work. Funders give to a social change organization because they believe in the mission—the work—of that organization. They believe the nonprofit offers a particular kind of value unavailable anywhere else, and funders certainly can't do that important work themselves or they wouldn't give you the money.

Therefore, to solve social problems it takes *both* solutions and money, in equal measure. You simply cannot have one without the other. So, as a nonprofit leader, you want to stop acting as if you would be lost without your funders. Because the truth is that they would also be lost without you.

Let me give you an example of what I mean. One of my clients, Van, is focused on solving a problem that the private sector helped create. Her nonprofit works to clean up the environmental messes that some corporations have created. Because a few of these corporate leaders recognize that they created the problem, and they are increasingly receiving negative press about it, they decided to invest in the solution Van offers.

But from the beginning, the partnership between these corporate funders and Van's nonprofit was unequal. Both Van and her corporate funders erroneously viewed these corporate investments as donations, and Van was expected to bend over backward to demonstrate the requisite gratitude.

In reality, Van offers a solution to a problem these corporate leaders are unable to solve on their own. The partnership between Van's nonprofit and these corporations could be infinitely more effective and powerful if both sides recognize the critical value that each brings to the table—corporations offering significant investment, and Van using that investment to create real, lasting change to a social problem they both want solved.

After several of our coaching conversations, Van began working with her corporate funders in a new way. She started to embrace the inherent equality in their working relationship. Thus empowered, she no longer felt afraid of them. She made small changes—such as approaching every meeting with her corporate funders with new confidence—and big shifts, like refusing to make compromising program changes that her corporate funders wanted. She even called a corporate leader's bluff when he threatened to pull funding if she didn't comply with a particular request that she felt undermined her program's integrity. She refused to make his requested change, and to Van's great surprise, the corporate funder stayed anyway.

A path toward an equal partnership with your funders comes from practicing some of the approaches we have discussed earlier in this book. When you reclaim your power, you begin to see that those around you, including your funders, are not better than but, rather, equal to you. Similarly, practicing compassion—for your funder as an investor and yourself as an investee—can create an equal partnership because it acknowledges the common humanity between you. When you recognize your funder as an imperfect investor of money and yourself as an imperfect implementer, you become equals. From this position of true equality a transformative social change partnership can form.

Another of my clients, Tim, was struggling to decide (at the behest of one of his key foundation funders) whether to expand his after-school program to a new school district. He was intrigued by the idea because a mix of circumstances (high need and proximity to other programs, among other things) had recently made investing in this school district popular among foundations.

But Tim was conflicted because, after years of experience implementing his successful program, he knew that this school district would not be a good fit for his program. The school district's leadership was not fully invested in Tim's approach, the district was located too far away for his staff to ensure program quality, and the expansion would stretch Tim's staff thin. Despite the drawbacks, Tim was seriously considering expanding to this new district simply because that key funder was keen to see Tim's program there.

This was a recipe for disaster, and I told Tim so. His desire to bend to his funder's whims would potentially compromise his program, his staff, and, most importantly, the students they worked with. An expansion to the new school district would actually decrease his nonprofit's ability to achieve their desired outcomes because (1) they were unlikely to achieve those outcomes with the new students (for all of the reasons outlined above), and (2) the additional drain on his staff would likely decrease the outcomes they were already achieving with their current students. If Tim kept quiet he would be doing both his mission and the foundation a disservice by keeping his expertise out of the equation.

I coached Tim on how to be open and honest with his funder and fully explain why expanding was a bad idea. I encouraged him to have this conversation from a place of equality with the funder. After their discussion, the funder completely understood and stopped pressuring Tim to move into the district.

I'm not suggesting that every funder will be this enlightened or that every funder will react positively when you approach them as an equal, but it is far better to lose a funder who doesn't have your mission at heart or isn't an equal partner than to have your work thrown off course.

Any partnership is infinitely more successful when it is forged among equal entities coming together to create value. This is true for all the partnerships you forge: with your funders, board members, advocates, policymakers—anyone with whom you work to achieve your mission. You form equal partnerships only when you truly value yourself, your organization, and the gifts you offer our world.

Create a Powerful Funding Ask

Once you recognize your true equality with current and prospective funders, you can then ensure that your messaging reflects this, to abundant effect.

If your fundraising message—whether a grant proposal, an email campaign, a major donor meeting, or an earned income venture pitch—comes from a place of feeling unworthy of or unequal to those whose investment you seek, you are divorcing yourself from your power as a confident, valuable, and equal social change warrior. And if your fundraising message makes you want to crawl into a hole, yawn, or tune out, it will be far worse for your prospective funders.

Instead, channel abundance (at every level) when you put together your fundraising message. Fully embrace the social value of your organization, your worth as a person asking for investment in its work, and the humanity of the person you are asking to write a check. Make your fundraising message expansive, exciting—even thrilling. Let it give you goosebumps, make you want to jump up and down, feel sexy and energized.

One of my clients, Jill, a nonprofit leader working at the forefront of political reform, is a poster child for nonprofit leaders doubting their value. Her nonprofit's contributions to strengthening our American democracy are clear to see... by everybody but her. She is so focused on the daily grind that she rarely, if ever, pokes her head up to see how much she and her organization contribute to our society—let alone declares that value to funders, policymakers, and partners. But, as I have told Jill, that has to stop. Over several coaching sessions, she and I worked together to uncover and announce the true value her organization creates. Armed with this definitive list of her organization's worth, Jill transformed the way she talked to, emailed, called, and spoke in front of all her funders. She has reached the point where, when she leaves meetings with funders, a palpable electricity of inspiration and excitement bubbles among them, which often translates into big checks. That's powerful.

When you approach any communication with your funders from an expansive, worthy, and inspiring position, your ability to attract abundance will grow.

Another client, Mavis, who is the CEO of a juvenile justice nonprofit, was preparing to make a larger ask to an ongoing funder. Mavis has been running an extremely effective, results-driven nonprofit for years. Because she and her team had been so successful, they and their board felt compelled to significantly grow.

I helped them create a strategy that would see them tripling their services (and thus their budget) over the next four years. Mavis, her board, and her staff were thrilled about this bigger vision. But when it came time for Mavis to approach funders for greater investments to realize it, she faltered. Despite her nonprofit's successes and their exciting plans for growth, Mavis still doubted her organization's ability to do more, and whether she could spend an additional investment wisely. At its core, her worry was that her organization was unworthy of greater investment.

Mavis and I had a heart-to-heart where I helped her see, and admit out loud, how much her organization has accomplished, how valuable it is to the children it serves and to the larger solution of keeping them from a lifetime of incarceration. She eventually got there, but she, probably like you, needed convincing.

I imagine that you have similar blinders on when it comes to the work of your nonprofit. So take a big step back and recognize the tremendous social value that you and your organization are contributing to the world. Then make your ask from the secure knowledge that your work—the work for which you need investment—has tremendous value.

And note: I don't use that word "investment" lightly. If you are truly working to create positive social change, donations simply are not going to cut it. You need real, significant, lasting investments. When you ask your funders to "give" or "donate," you are putting your organization's work squarely back in the charity camp we discussed in chapter one. You don't want your funders to "do you a favor" by donating. Rather, you want funders to invest in your strategy, your programs, your social change vision. You want them to be equal partners in the work of creating a better world.

To give you some ideas of the importance of language (which reveals your mindset and intention) in raising money,

I have transformed some common fundraising messages into more powerful, abundant asks:

"Donate to our cause" becomes
"invest in our solution."

"Become a donor" shifts to
"become our partner in the work."

"Help us reach our goals" transforms
to "join us in creating change."

"We need money" becomes
"invest in this opportunity."

The language of the second phrases is expansive rather than restrictive, centered in abundance rather than in scarcity. If the message you use to ask others to fund your work comes from a place of worth, equality, and joy, then that abundance will follow.

Money can become your friend. It can become a powerful tool for achieving the social change you seek. But it requires that you eschew the typical nonprofit fundraising approach in favor of a more robust social change financing approach.

Abundance doesn't just include money. An abundance of people are trying to reach you as well. Let's figure out how to mobilize your inside team and outside network.

5

Mobilize Your Inside Team and Outside Network

———

"That is happiness; to be dissolved into something complete and great. When it comes to one, it comes as naturally as sleep."

WILLA CATHER

THE EXECUTIVE DIRECTOR of a nonprofit aimed at getting more women in positions of power in the financial markets, Nita, called me one day because she was struggling with the usual list of nonprofit concerns: a disengaged board, a budget shortfall, an exhausted staff, a limited network of influencers. She couldn't figure out how to move beyond never having enough but desperately wanted to achieve so much more. Her worldview was pretty bleak.

She couldn't see the potential connections that were staring her right in the face. There were organizations, networks, experts, movements, even money—yes, money!—sitting on the sidelines, waiting for her to connect. I could see them all. But she could not.

Social change leaders often unnecessarily isolate themselves by believing that no one else shares their unique burden, that no one else understands exactly what they are going through, that no one else can help. I find myself stuck believing it's all up to me sometimes, too. As humans we all feel, at one time or another, that we are desperately alone. This sense of isolation is particularly true for social change leaders, for many reasons. To name a few:

- The scarcity mindset of the social change sector makes you (wrongly) believe that there is fierce competition for limited resources, which discourages you from seeking cooperation, collaboration, and connection.

- The lack of value placed on social change efforts has convinced you that you should deny yourself whatever you really need.

- The overhead myth keeps you from seeking funding and paying enough for the staff and systems your social change goals truly require, resulting in never having enough help.

This false belief that you are on your own creates not only loneliness and exhaustion, but also, and more tragically, less social change.

So, to move from the lonely, exhausting place of isolation to the energizing, connected place of abundant social change, view yourself as the ultimate connector—a connector of those outside and inside your organization's walls. When you embrace your role as a connector of disparate groups, organizations, and networks to something bigger than what you or your organization alone can accomplish; when you understand yourself as the leader of a movement of social change warriors, you will accomplish so much more.

Where Do You Need Help?

The first step is admitting where you need help. This very act will first, and most importantly, open the possibility in your mind that you can't do it all alone. Second, it will begin to direct that help to you. To figure out where you need help, answer these questions:

- Do you have access to enough money to feel confident in your ability to achieve the social change your organization is working toward?

- Do you feel that the ultimate burden for achieving your mission is carried by more people than just you?

- Do you have a competent, savvy group of advisors (staff, board, colleagues, peers) that you can regularly turn to for advice, insight, and support?

- Do you view those your organization serves as equal partners in the work and regularly engage them in program development?

- Do you have enough confidence in your staff that you can easily delegate large pieces of the work?

- Do you feel that your board is actively and productively engaged in moving your organization's work forward?

- Do you feel deeply connected to other leaders in your space and regularly turn to them for advice and support?

- Is your organization actively partnering with other entities at a deep level?

- Do you regularly analyze how your space (the people you serve, other organizations, demographic and cultural shifts) is changing over time?

A "no" to any of these questions is an area where you can focus on mobilizing your network, both inside and outside your organization.

In the many years I've been working with social change leaders, I have come to realize that one simple thing separates organizations that create lasting social change from those that don't: critical mass. Critical mass means you have enough influencers, funders, decision-makers, experts, board members, staff, and volunteers aligned in their desire to achieve some social change. "Enough" is a subjective term, by design. There is no magic number, but I assure you that it is greater than one.

So often when I talk to a social change leader for the first time, I will see opportunities for her to make powerful, transformative connections for her nonprofit—to influencers, networks, organizations, trends, advocates, money, even her own board and staff—which she just doesn't see. A critical mass out there longs to be marshaled. I would bet that connections out there are ready to help you do so much more, too. You just can't see them, *yet*.

You have the power to marshal those inside your walls (clients, board, staff) and those outside your walls (funders, collaborators, partners, influencers) toward your social change goals. The key is to see yourself as the linchpin connecting disparate people, partners, money, momentum, and energy to an exciting, inspiring, and game-changing common social change goal. That is the true art of this work.

So, first let's find those powerful connections waiting for you inside your own walls.

The key is to see yourself as the linchpin connecting disparate people, partners, money, momentum, and energy to an exciting, inspiring, and game-changing common social change goal.

Mobilize Your Inside Team

The state of support inside most nonprofits is pretty sad. It usually goes something like this: a disengaged, dysfunctional board poorly leads a financially strapped, exhausted, and underappreciated staff. Harsh, but fairly true.

If I just described your organization, take heart, because it doesn't have to be that way. Inside your nonprofit's walls are abundant productive connections likely just waiting for you to mobilize them.

Partner with your target populations

Let's start with your organization's target populations. Recall from the Theory of Change in chapter three that your organization's target populations are those your organization seeks to benefit or influence. For example, if you lead a social service nonprofit this would be your clients; if you run an advocacy organization this would be policymakers.

As we have discussed, rather than taking a charity approach, which creates an unequal relationship between the giver of services and the receiver of those services, instead see your target populations as powerful change agents themselves. Fully integrate them into the work. Regularly connect with your target populations to understand what they need, what's working, what's not. Ask them to develop their role in the social change you are creating together.

A client of mine, Javier, is CEO of a nonprofit organization that works to create an equitable playing field for low-income students in middle and high school. Javier understands integrating the students themselves into the work is a big way to achieve the organization's goals. So, they have created an impressive structure of self-directed student groups that advise the organization on every aspect of its programs. In essence, the students themselves help create the programs that serve them.

How powerful is that? The benefits are enormous—the programs are more effective because they are informed by the students' experience and knowledge, and the structure of program development itself provides the students opportunities for self-empowerment and determination. At the same time, the burden of social change doesn't rest solely on the shoulders of Javier's board and staff. It is instead fully shared work.

When you open the work of your organization to those you benefit or influence, the burdens lift and the work becomes more effective.

Elevate your board

Ah, the board. The thorn in the side of so many social change leaders.

It's an odd system, if you think about it. The head staff member of a social change organization is hired and evaluated by a group of volunteers who, as such, have many higher priorities vying for their time and attention. This head staff member, in turn, must work tirelessly to keep each of her volunteer bosses engaged and productive for a handful of years until they each roll off the board, while she helps identify, train, and engage the next batch of recruits. What a Sisyphean task!

But it doesn't have to be that way. Call me a hopeless optimist (you wouldn't be the first), but I see a dysfunctional, disengaged board as a missed opportunity to elevate it to the level that your social change work requires. A highly functioning board can be a huge asset to a nonprofit—expanding the organization's network, influence, expertise, and access to money, among other things. I promise, you can create a productive board that becomes a critical part of your team.

The first step is to fully embrace the idea that asking someone to join your board is a huge opportunity for them. Yes, you read that correctly. Serving your organization and your social change work is an opportunity, not a burden, for your board member.

Think about it. If you were approached by an impressive and committed group of people who believed that you possess some unique and invaluable characteristics required to move their goals forward, and you believe in moving those goals forward, wouldn't you be honored to climb aboard? Wouldn't you be exhilarated by the opportunity to put your talents to work for something big and exciting? Of course you would.

That is exactly how you want to approach potential board members—offering them an opportunity to use their important and unique talents to achieve a greater good. So, when you are recruiting new board members and working with your current board members, fully embrace the tremendous value you, your organization, and your social change work are offering them. With that powerful mindset, you can then assemble the right board members and guide each one to put their unique gifts to use.

Recruit the board you actually need to achieve your social change goals, not the one that shows up by default. As we have been discussing throughout this book, the more you articulate what you want, the more likely you are to get it.

If you can be crystal clear about the skills, experience, and networks you need your board members to possess, you are much more likely to find board members with those traits.

To do this, take a hard look at each goal of your organization's strategic plan and answer the question:

"What skills, experience, and networks do we need at the board level to achieve our long-term strategy?"

For example, if you lead a school-based literacy nonprofit, you might need board members to open doors to school district decision-makers. That means you need at least one or two of your board members to have strong relationships with those decision-makers. Thinking through the goals of your strategic plan, you might come up with the first few characteristics of your desired board like this:

- skills: "ability to understand and analyze literacy interventions";
- experience: "experience growing organizations";
- networks: "connections to school district decision-makers"

... and so on. Once you've created your list of desired board skills, experience, and networks, analyze each of your current board members to see which of the desired traits are already present in your current members and which are not. The qualities you've listed that few to no board members possess (the area circled in the diagram below) are exactly the skills, experience, and networks your new board recruits must have. This process allows you to align your board to your organization's goals and be targeted about the characteristics of new board members. Knowing what you are looking for, you can then ask your current board, your funders, your partners—anyone and everyone—to connect you to people who possess those specific characteristics.

Board Skills, Experience, and Networks Matrix

BOARD MEMBER	ABILITY TO UNDERSTAND LITERACY INTERVENTIONS	EXPERIENCE GROWING ORGS	CONNECTIONS TO SCHOOL DECISION-MAKERS
Joe Burns	X		X
Mathilda Mathis			
Amy Clark			X
Jesus Garza	X		

This process is also useful for better engaging your current board members. If you can show individual board members what you need them to uniquely contribute to your vision, they will become more energized. Most of us ultimately want to see our unique gifts contribute to something much bigger— to be "dissolved into something complete and great," to use Willa Cather's line from this chapter's epigraph. So, you must help each board member understand how his unique and valuable gifts, if put to use, will be instrumental in bringing your social change vision to fruition.

You can do this by meeting one-on-one at least annually with each board member to discuss their specific contributions to the organization, rather than leaving their engagement up to the happenstance of board meetings. In these one-on-one meetings, you can ask questions to move each board member toward deeper engagement and productivity:

- **"Why do you serve?"** This question does two things. First, it forces your board member to tap into her unique reasons for agreeing to be on the board. Ideally, she has a passion for the mission. Answering this question reconnects her with what drives her to show up. Second, it gives you more details about what energizes her so you can focus on those things to further engage her.

- **"What results are we achieving?"** This can be a real opportunity to get your board member excited about where the organization is going and the value it provides the world. His excitement can fuel a desire to do more to realize that vision.

- **"What skills, experience, and networks can you bring to our work?"** This question opens the door to a discussion of the powerful, unique gifts your board member could bring to bear. You can offer your view of what her talents are, and she can offer hers. Together, you can figure out how to tap into her specific assets.

- **"How do you want to contribute this year?"** This is where the magic happens. You take the specific assets you uncovered in the last question and work together to turn them into measurable, productive action. Ask your board member to be specific: "I will secure meetings with three education leaders I know" or "I will look at your growth model and ask hard questions." Make sure that his contributions include both mission and money—you don't want to make the mistake of divesting any board member of his role in your financial model.

Capture what you and each board member agree to in these meetings, and share your notes with them, respectively. Use them to, together, monitor progress throughout the year.

You can also use these notes to give helpful nudges to board members whose energy wanes as the year wears on. If a board member isn't meeting the contributions you both agreed on, you must address the situation. This is critical to the engagement of the rest of the board. The very real risk in keeping a troublesome board member is that his presence will put a damper on the rest of the board's energy and productivity. If a board member is missing in action, meddling where she shouldn't, not delivering on her agreed upon contributions, or otherwise being unproductive or unhelpful, deal with it quickly. Meet with the errant board member (either by yourself or, better yet, with your board chair) and create a plan and timeline for improvement. If she doesn't improve how and when she says she will, ask her to resign. If you are allergic to confrontations like this, the book *Crucial Conversations* can show you how to build your muscle for difficult conversations with board members.[1] (And staff, funders— even spouses and children!)

Beyond engaging each board member individually, you can also more productively engage them as a group. Lead meetings that focus less on informing the board and more on involving them in energizing, expansive, abundant, strategic discussions that tap into their abilities and help them to move your goals forward. Remember, board members want to see that their contributions have value. Asking people to sit around listening to staff drone on doesn't do that. Instead, whenever the board gets together, find ways (and carve out time) to provoke thoughtful discussion, brainstorm new ideas, and/or plan for the future.

You elevate your board to become the team you need by viewing them as a partner in a shared vision. Instead of fearing, dismissing, growing frustrated by, or simply surviving your board until a better one comes along, make them a qualified, engaged, and productive part of your team.

Empower your staff

As with your board, the way you start building the staff you truly need is by adopting the right mindset. You have to believe that your organization is worthy of hiring, developing, managing, and leading the staff you require to accomplish the social change you seek.

In the social change sector, the words "leading" and "managing" are sometimes tossed around interchangeably. But they are two very different, and equally necessary, elements of achieving abundant social change.

A *leader* provides an inspiring, motivating big vision for the staff and board to get behind. She asks hard questions and constantly pushes the organization and its people to try harder, reach higher, think bigger. A leader makes sure that people are engaged and invested in the work and creates a team environment where each person feels part of something much larger than herself. In this way, a leader inspires people to do more and be more than they ever thought possible.

A *manager* creates systems that allow the organization to get things done and holds the board and staff accountable. He makes sure that everyone knows what they are doing, has the tools they need to get the job done, and is held responsible for their part. A manager executes the path that a leader has articulated.

So, in an ideal scenario, the leader and manager work as a perfect team. One strategizes, propels, and inspires. The other creates systems and accountability to bring the strategy to fruition. Sometimes, in larger organizations, the leader and the manager will be contained in two different people, or in several people (senior management team, board chair, and CEO). Other times, the executive director of a small organization may need to play the role of leader and manager in equal measure. It doesn't matter if these roles are contained in one person or multiple people, as long as everyone understands which is which, and when.

Beyond who is leading and managing in your organization, it is also helpful to understand who performs which function. There are typically three broad staff functions in a social change organization:

- **Program development and delivery.** The person or team who creates and delivers the mission-related "products and services" of your organization.

- **External support.** The person or team who creates and executes the strategy for bringing money in the door. Ideally this role includes marketing and communications, as well, since their primary function is to bring more external support (in all forms) to the organization.

- **Administration.** The person or team who develops and manages the internal systems such as human resources, technology, finance and accounting.

You don't necessarily have to employ at least three people in your organization. But you do want each of these areas staffed in a way that allows you to execute your long-term plans.

Just as you determined what your board needs to look like to deliver on your organization's strategic plan, do the same at the staff level. Go through your strategic plan, and ask:

"What staff positions do we need so that we can deliver on each goal of our long-term strategy?"

Sometimes you may not be able to determine this on your own. If that is the case, an organizational assessment (which we discussed in the previous chapter) might help you understand how to structure and potentially grow your staff to meet your long-term goals.

Once you understand what staff positions you require, commit to paying whatever it takes to get the best people. As we discussed in chapter four, a classic scarcity-based nonprofit refrain is, "We don't have enough money to hire top talent." Don't fall into the trap of hiring someone with less experience than the position requires because it's cheaper.

Instead hire (and pay for) someone who can take the position to the next level. Then create a budget that accommodates those salary levels, raising capacity capital (as we discussed in chapter four) if necessary.

Once you have recruited the best and brightest to your staff, fully empower them to do their best work. Just as you identified where to focus your time through the zones of competence exercise in chapter two, ask the rest of your staff to do the same. Then help them figure out how to delegate the responsibilities on their zones of incompetence and competence lists.

Keep in mind that the scarcity mindset sometimes translates to an inability to delegate effectively. Perhaps because social change leaders are so used to going it alone, they often think that delegation just isn't viable. To buck this trend, schedule a weekly, one-on-one meeting with each of your direct reports that focuses on your goals for their position. This gives your staff ample leeway to shine, while allowing you to help overcome hurdles and monitor progress along the way. These one-on-ones also create fewer interruptions during the rest of the week because your staff knows they predictably have your dedicated attention—all of which creates an empowered staff, a confident leader, and a productive organization.

If, along the way, you find that a particular staff member isn't performing as you would like, you can set clear expectations for improvement. If those expectations still aren't met, you can help the staff member move on to something (either inside or outside your organization) that is a better fit for their own brand of genius. Once you recruit (and pay for) top performers and simultaneously empower and support them, you create an army of energized, engaged, and abundant staff members.

Now let's focus on gathering the team that is waiting for you outside your organization's walls.

Mobilize Your Outside Network

In their 2008 article in the *Stanford Social Innovation Review*, network experts Jane Wei-Skillern and Sonia Marciano articulated the concept of a "networked nonprofit," which their research showed is much more effective at creating social change than the traditional nonprofit approach. Networked nonprofits think of themselves as "nodes within a constellation of equal, interconnected partners, rather than as hubs at the center of their nonprofit universes." They break down their own walls and work toward social change in a large, collaborative way.[2]

Similarly, in a follow-up article, Jane Wei-Skillern, David Ehrlichman, and David Sawyer describe a "network entrepreneur" as fundamentally different from, and much more effective at creating social change than, a traditional nonprofit leader, because "the potential for impact increases exponentially when leaders leverage resources of all types— leadership, money, talent—across organizations and sectors toward a common goal."[3]

In essence, the networked approach to social change is one where you put aside your ego, and the ego of your organization, to gather all the necessary experts, funders, influencers, collaborators, and institutions and mobilize them toward a shared vision of social change. Instead of leading only an organization, as a "network entrepreneur" you lead a social change effort that includes many and diverse people and organizations. A network entrepreneur understands that social change lives beyond any single organization. It requires someone (or a set of someones) to create a larger vision for social change, marshal all the necessary resources, and lead people toward that vision.

This concept is critical to social change leaders, who often believe that they work within a scarce system. If embraced, the networked approach could transform your work. If instead of working to build an institution, you worked to build networks, you could be much more effective at creating abundant social change.

But what does that look like? How do you become more "networked"?

The networked approach to social change means taking a big step back from the work you have always done and asking a much broader set of questions. It means having an abundance worldview, believing that you and your organization could be a part of something much larger. It means plugging into other leaders and organizations that recognize how together you can do so much more. To do this, let's look at each category of the team outside your walls:

- collaborators and competitors;
- current and potential funders;
- industry and solution experts; and
- policy influencers.

Collaborators and competitors

I know that, in the social change sector, the word "competitor" is a naughty one. Nonprofit leaders are often encouraged by funders and others to view everyone as a "collaborator." The (erroneous) idea is that if we are all trying to make the world a better place, there should be no room for competition, only collaboration. The truth is much more complicated.

If social change leaders become crystal clear about their unique contributions to a social problem, distinct from the contributions of others in the field, each can have a larger effect on the social problem. So, the concept of competition has real value for the sector because it forces each social change entity to figure out what it does best and how that fits (or doesn't) with what similar entities are also doing.

If, aided by your board, staff, and some market research (which I'll discuss in greater detail below) you can determine your organization's core competencies, you can identify how to contribute more effectively to the larger network of social change efforts beyond your walls. Recall that your core competencies are what you do better than anyone else—capabilities, expertise, assets, or connections that your organization uniquely possesses. They are strengths on steroids. Remember to resist the common urge to name a lot of core competencies. Any single organization usually has only a short list of things (two to five) that could truly be considered core competencies.

A social change organization will be most successful at creating sustainable social change when it works on a *social problem* (or set of problems) that its *core competencies* uniquely position it to address, apart from its *competitors or collaborators*.

Let me be clear. I am not arguing against collaboration. The exact opposite is the case. The goal is greater collaboration. But when they collaborate, the board and staff must understand exactly what their organization brings to the table that is unique from what others are bringing. In this way, you can be crystal clear about the value you add, as distinct from the value others add, to the social change you all seek.

Once you know this, reaching out to others in your field is much easier and more effective. So often I see social change leaders who are all working (either tangentially or directly) on a similar set of social issues but rarely finding ways to truly connect with each other. Once you've determined your core competencies, you can connect with your "competitors" and "collaborators" to find opportunities to share the social change burden. I know that the scarcity mindset often makes outreach to a potential competitor difficult because of fear of losing advantages or resources. But there is more than enough money and resources for you and your competitors and your collaborators, as long as you all do work that provides value.

Instead of competing against each other in your silos, you can articulate what each of you uniquely brings to the table and then forge deep and effective partnerships to be stronger together. And I don't mean traditional nonprofit partnerships that are short term and involve creating and implementing a single program. Rather, I am talking about long-term, strategic alliances.

Let me explain how this worked for one of my clients. Eleanor is the head of a network of organizations focused on elevating women's voices in media—news, entertainment, and social media. Their Theory of Change is that if media includes more women-centered stories, women will feel more empowered to seek and achieve more positions of power in society overall. The problem, when they came to me, was that they had big plans for impacting the enormous world of media, but a small budget and limited access to media gatekeepers and decision-makers. Although they had some partnerships with organizations beyond their network, these were limited and often involved a corporation donating a few thousand dollars to sponsor one of their events. I encouraged Eleanor and her partners to think much, much bigger about how to create powerful strategic alliances with large global companies. These affiliations would go far beyond typical corporate donations. We envisioned a savvy joint effort that ultimately integrated one network into much larger networks and audiences.

We brainstormed large corporations that had a business interest in adult women and put together a pitch about how this network and these corporations were aligned. Then, using LinkedIn, Eleanor had her team research the staff and board members on our list of prospective corporations and cross-researched those with the names of board members and close donors of her network. The idea was to find people in her current network who were connected to decision-makers at the prospective corporate partners. Whenever they found a match, they asked their person to introduce them to the corporate decision-maker. Eleanor then pitched the corporations for a significant financial investment along with ways to work together to share audiences and platforms to elevate and empower more women. Although not every corporation they met with wanted to partner, some did, and those strategic alliances helped dramatically grow Eleanor's financial model, audience, and reach.

Once you see other leaders and organizations out there as potential allies—true collaborators—you realize that the enormous burden of social change resting on your shoulders can be shared.

Outside experts

Beyond other entities that might share your goals for social change, there are also likely people who have expertise that could make your work easier or more effective.

It takes courage for a social change leader to admit when she doesn't know something. A few years ago I heard a fascinating interview with Leah Hager Cohen, who wrote the book *I Don't Know*. She describes the freedom that comes from admitting that you just don't know something. That moment of honesty can lead to transformation: "Once you finally own up to what you don't know, then you can begin to have honest interactions with the people around you."[4] When you have the courage to admit that you don't know how to do everything, you open yourself, and your social change work, to finding the expertise you may need.

As we discussed, a single organization's list of core competencies is limited, and chances are the social change you seek requires additional expertise that your organization does not possess. There are likely experts inside and outside your social change area who could offer key knowledge that could propel your work forward.

The trick is adopting a "beginner's mind"—the Zen Buddhist concept of *shoshin*—which is to approach things (even things that you have deep experience with) as a beginner would, with an attitude of openness, eagerness, and lack of preconceptions.[5] When you open your social change work to the expansive, abundant idea that you don't already have all the possible answers but that the answers are yet to be found, you open your work to so much more.

An expert can be anyone with knowledge or experience that could be helpful to a problem you face. My favorite example of finding expertise in unlikely places is biomimicry. Biomimicry is "a method for creating solutions to human challenges by emulating designs and ideas found in nature."[6] It is the (revolutionary!) idea that nature has expertise that we can employ to solve problems in areas that we humans face. There are countless examples of solutions designed by mimicking nature—bullet trains, wind turbines, and camouflage, to name a few.

When you imagine that an answer to a challenge might exist outside your organization, your issue area, your industry, or your sector, you open yourself to novel and exciting solutions. Think about these questions to determine where you might find some missing expertise to propel you forward:

- Could approaches used to address other social issues provide insight to your work?

- Are there effective models of something similar in the for-profit sector?

- What different industries employ novel approaches or use new tools that might be applicable to your work?

- Do key for-profit industries or local, state, or federal government entities have insight into your set of social problems?

- Do any demographic, economic, and cultural shifts intersect with your organization's work?

Once you are aware of what expertise you desire, you can use your network (staff, board, funders, consultants, partners) to find people who can introduce you to these experts, and thus open your organization and your work to a more expansive set of solutions.

Current and potential funders

You can also open your social change work to the expansive potential of more and different kinds of funders. Making your current funders equal partners in the work will go a long way to bolstering the funders section of your growing network. In addition, you can cast a wider net for potential funders.

Often social changemakers view their list of potential funding sources in a limited way. Several years ago, Christina, the executive director of a nonprofit that provides social services to individuals who are homeless, approached me. Her organization's revenue completely relied on individuals and foundations that had an interest in homelessness. As a result, her budget was smaller than she wanted it to be, and not diversified. I encouraged Christina to think about funders in a much broader sense, about all the people and entities that benefitted when Christina's programs were successful. With a broader understanding of who could find value in the solutions Christina's nonprofit offered, she and her staff began approaching several local businesses that had expressed concern about people who were homeless camping in front of their businesses. Christina convinced them to invest as partners in the food, housing, and job training programs her nonprofit offered. This new fundraising approach opened up a whole new corporate support arm for Christina's organization, and revenue grew dramatically.

It is critical not to put your organization and your social change work in a box. Think more expansively about the solutions you offer. Rather than assuming that only a small category of funders will be interested in your work, believe that a much larger cross section of funders share your goals. When my clients embrace a more abundant view of who can benefit from their solutions, greater funding often follows.

So, before you assume that you have exhausted the list of who could potentially fund your work, ask the question:

> ## "Who are all the people or groups who will benefit if our work is successful?"

I'm not suggesting you make connections that simply aren't there. Rather I am encouraging you to see the potential funding connections by widening your scope.

Policy influencers

The last piece of the team waiting outside your walls may be people who can influence policy that affects your social change work.

As we discussed in chapter one, social change organizations have historically been told to stay out of politics and lobbying. Thus, many social change leaders and board members have feared a public policy role for their organizations. But 501(c)(3) organizations can absolutely get involved in political and legal battles that impact their mission. Tim Delaney, CEO of the National Council of Nonprofits, has argued in recent years that advocacy is "a profound responsibility and effective tool to advance nonprofit missions."[7] Similarly, according to the Council on Foundations, private, public, and community foundations can legally play a much bigger role in advocacy than most currently do.[8]

If the social problem your organization addresses is itself impacted by a larger system, include policy influencers as part of your outside team.

Analyze local, state, or federal policies that might impact your work. Brainstorm the policymakers and policy influencers you can connect to, to make sure they fully understand the issues and their impact. Talk with journalists who cover those policy beats. They could likely give you ideas and perhaps write about your organization's viewpoint. If you don't know how to find out who the policy influencers might be and how to mobilize them, both the National Council of Nonprofits[9] and the Council on Foundations[10] have great tools and resources to start moving into the advocacy space.

Conducting market research

To connect to and mobilize the team outside your walls, you have to physically go outside your walls. To be more networked, and thus more abundant at creating social change, you must understand the external space in which you operate. And to understand it, you must investigate it.

Ongoing market research can help you understand what your target populations need; what your competitors and collaborators are doing, and where they might be going; what demographic or cultural shifts experts foresee; what potential funders want now and in the future; how policy approaches might help your work; and how the very problems you exist to solve might be changing over time.

By "market research" I don't mean expensive, time-consuming, rigorous data gathering. I mean things like:

- one-on-one calls with funders to understand their interests, future plans, and needs;

- one-on-one meetings with collaborators to hear their views on how the industry or social issues are changing over time, and what they need;

- interviews with industry or domain experts to understand how they see the problem changing over time;

- interviews with researchers whose work applies to yours to understand what they are learning;

- internet research on competitors to learn how they are adapting, growing, planning, and being funded; and

- online surveys of your target populations to understand their needs, how they might be changing over time, and what they would like to see from you.

The clients I work with find that having these kinds of conversations and uncovering this information, which transforms how they see and interact with the world outside their walls, is hugely beneficial. Beyond the critical knowledge you will gain when conducting market research, there is another huge benefit to this data gathering—it forces you to expand and strengthen your network. Because in the act of finding out what's happening outside your walls, you will forge new and deeper connections with the people beyond them.

Once you've figured out all the people and groups you want to connect with, involve your board and staff. Remember, it's not all up to you! Set up meetings to explore how you can start partnering toward bigger social change. And make sure you approach those meetings in an open, networked way. Not everyone will want to share information or partner with you, and that's okay. The new alliances you form and the information you gather can be transformational.

As you begin to engage with the teams both inside and outside your walls, the more excited about your organization and its social change work your staff, board, funders, partners, influencers, and experts will become. Forging new and more connections begets new and more connections. The more often you think about and interact with the bigger world, the more you create an abundance of people, organizations, influencers, experts, money, energy, and excitement flowing toward your work.

Rather than viewing yourself as the only one who can do the work the right way, consider yourself the connector of a vast web of people and resources, all working toward a big, common vision for social change. In gathering and guiding others well, you let go and trust that they (your board, staff, partners, funders, and allies) will make good choices and do good work. You will accomplish so much more if you guide the work of an abundant many, rather than relying on the work of a scarce few.

It is only in connecting—to fellow social change warriors, to the transformative energy of money, to experts and advocates, to influencers and friends—that you will realize the social change you seek.

Conclusion: Change Yourself, Change the System, Change the World

"We are the ones
we've been waiting for."

JUNE JORDAN

ECENTLY I RAN into a client I had worked with many years ago. Although I had kept up with Joan intermittently via email, I hadn't been in her presence for at least three years. When I saw her across the room, I almost didn't recognize her. She had obviously been exercising and eating well because she was much trimmer than I remembered. She also had a smart haircut and was wearing a beautiful, well-fitting suit. But what struck me the most was the glow of happiness and peace that emanated from her. Her eyes were clear, her smile enormous. She seemed very at ease in her own skin.

This was such a shock to me because when I first met Joan more than ten years ago she looked completely different. She was exhausted, her skin had a grayish pallor, and her eyes continually darted around the room. She had trouble focusing, sitting still, and making clear decisions. She was perpetually terrified about making payroll for the college readiness nonprofit she ran. Her staff was completely disillusioned with her inability to make decisions, to raise money, to recruit and wrangle the board. Her organization was hemorrhaging money and needed to shut down some of its programs to make ends meet. Joan was desperate to find a better way.

I began by conducting an organizational assessment to determine where the organization lacked capacity. I discovered that almost every aspect of the organization was locked in scarcity. From a poorly paid staff with high turnover to a disengaged board to an overreliance on limited foundation funding to weak program delivery infrastructure, Joan's organization was struggling. In a lengthy report, I explained to the board and staff how, over the next few years, they could move each aspect of the organization to a much more abundant place. I then led them to create a three-year strategic plan and a growing, diversified financial model. Finally, I spent a year coaching Joan, her board, and her staff about how to navigate the many organizational changes contained in this ambitious strategic plan. When I left them, they were well on their way. Her board was much more engaged in strategy and fundraising, and their revenue sources had grown, allowing them to hire new staff and expand their programs.

But the changes continued long after I left. With a new worldview that any challenge could be turned into an opportunity, Joan and her organization blossomed. And more interestingly, I later learned, Joan became an example to many of her fellow nonprofit leaders. Seeing what she had accomplished, they wanted to "know her secret." Joan's transformation also affected the leaders of the secondary schools and colleges with which her organization partnered. They, too, learned by osmosis Joan's more abundant approach, and they started, often unconsciously, to adopt it.

Today Joan is not only a more empowered, joyful, abundant nonprofit leader, but she has also inspired a catalytic shift toward abundance in the people with whom she regularly interacts. And each one of those people has their own sphere of influence that they may have moved, however slightly, toward a more abundant worldview.

I know that you, in all your endless humility, find it difficult to absorb the idea that you can have the same kind of influence as Joan. The vast majority of social change leaders barely feel worthy of the change their organizations are attempting to achieve, let alone worthy of impacting the broken system of social change overall.

But the actions of a single person can have an enormous ripple effect. Each one of us has a far greater impact on the world around us than we could ever fathom. And that influence swings much more toward the positive when we embrace an abundant worldview.

I want more for you because you deserve it. You are inspiring to behold. You give me faith in humankind every single day. The world desperately needs the amazing solutions you have to offer.

More importantly, I want more for you because if you feel more supported, more powerful, more abundant, you will spread those solutions far and wide. You will remake your organization and our broken systems, cities, communities, and world. You will transform those broken systems into stronger, healthier, equitable ones.

As we emerge from a global pandemic, we will have much work to do, and we need true leaders to chart that path forward. The chaos of 2020 showed us that the most unlikely people can become true leaders, while those with big leadership titles can fail miserably. True leaders are not born, they are made. Leadership historian Nancy Koehn argues that leadership is not inherent in any one person; rather, leaders are created when they face a critical event and consciously decide to step up to the plate: "Leaders make themselves capable of doing extraordinary things." In this moment in time, as Koehn puts it, "We need great, courageous leaders like we need oxygen and water."[1]

Now is the time for true leaders to step up—and I don't mean just political leaders. It is in the social change sector, the sector that has always been about making the world a better place, where we can look for that leadership. So, be that leader. Courageously choose to build and grow your own breed of abundant social change by:

- recognizing that what weighs you down is based on outdated, limiting, and burdensome beliefs that you can move beyond;

- realizing that the power to overcome these burdens, gather people and money to your cause, and ultimately achieve the social change you seek already resides within you;

- understanding that although the work will be hard, it doesn't have to be defeating, and in fact it can be joyful and empowering;

- attracting all the money you could ever need to achieve your social change vision;

- knowing that you are so supported, in ways that you can see and ways that you cannot.

When you embrace social change abundance, you not only solve your own organization's woes, but you connect

When you embrace social change abundance, you not only solve your own organization's woes, but you connect your work to a force far greater than you alone. You become a leader not only in your own pocket of the world but of this Great Reset in which we now find ourselves.

your work to a force far greater than you alone. You create a new path forward for the social change sector. You become an example of an abundant social change leader, bringing abundant change to broken systems in an abundant world. You become a leader not only in your own pocket of the world but of this Great Reset in which we now find ourselves.

As a social change leader during a time when our institutions are crumbling, inequality pervades most of our systems, and our planet is in crisis, you have a unique opportunity to reinvent social change. But you must do the work very differently. You can recognize that the system in which you find yourself and your social change work is simply not functioning anymore. You can chart for yourself, and for the rest of us, a better way forward.

When you decide in a single moment to show up differently to your social change work, you serve as an example to other social change leaders. When you say, "no more!" to a scarcity-based system, you make it that much easier for the social changemaker who witnesses your brave act to say the same. When you empower yourself, you (often unknowingly) empower others. When you believe that abundance is truly possible, you help other social change leaders to believe in it, too. When you ask for help, you silently give permission for others to seek help themselves.

So stop dimming your light. Stop playing by the broken rules that have held you back for far too long. Stop denying the tremendous power you have within you. Stop choosing scarcity over the enormous abundance that is only waiting for you to open your arms. Stop treating money like a fiend, and embrace it as an ally in the work. Stop believing it is all up to you, and start connecting to all that wants to help you achieve the social change you seek.

You can choose how you do your social change work. You can choose how you lead your staff, your board, your funders, your partners, and your peers forward. You can choose to stay on the well-worn path of scarcity, or you can choose a more joyful, expansive way forward. In making that courageous choice, you are signaling to those around you a new way forward. You are showing them how to stop dimming their lights, too.

And this is how we create, brick by brick, a healthier, more equitable world. A world we always knew was possible. A world to behold.

"We are all just walking each other home."

RAM DASS

Acknowledgments

THIS BOOK IS far from mine alone. I had an amazing team of guides, helpers, supporters, friends, and family all along the way.

To the smart, savvy, supportive team at Page Two, who made writing this book such a joy.

To my brother, who is always with me and inspires me every single day.

To my walking buddies, who cheered me on every step of the way.

To Patty, who believed in me when I didn't.

To Mary, who launched my love of social change organizations so long ago and has provided many years of cheerleading since.

To sweet Sadie and Milo, for their endless love.

To my book club ladies, who make me think and laugh and constantly offer the amazing energy that emerges whenever kick-ass women assemble.

To my parents, who always encouraged me to speak my mind, ask hard questions, and never settle.

To Phil and Aileen, who have always offered such incredible love and support in everything I've ever done.

To all my clients over the years and their fellow social change warriors. I have learned so much from you and with you. Please know that you are angels on this earth, and you are a constant inspiration to me.

To my wonderful, supportive, whip-smart husband, who constantly finds the perfect balance between urging me out of my comfort zone and providing a soft place to land.

And finally, to my two amazing, thoughtful, passionate, and empathetic boys. They, and so many like them in their generation, give me such hope for a healthier, more equitable world.

Notes

Introduction

Epigraph: Steven Pressfield, *The War of Art: Break Through the Blocks and Win Your Inner Creative Battles* (New York: Black Irish Entertainment, LLC, 2002).

Chapter One

Epigraph: Barack Obama, "Barack Obama's Caucus Speech," *New York Times*, January 3, 2008, https://www.nytimes.com/2008/01/03/us/politics/03obama-transcript.html.

1   "Gaslighting," *Psychology Today*, accessed August 28, 2020, https://www.psychologytoday.com/us/basics/gaslighting.

2   Robert M. Penna, "How 'Charity' Became 'Philanthropy,'" *Stanford Social Innovation Review*, September 4, 2018, https://ssir.org/books/excerpts/entry/how_charity_became_philanthropy.

3   Robert Egger, "A New Generation, a New Commitment to Change," *The Chronicle of Philanthropy*, January 24, 2008, http://www.robertegger.org/wp-content/uploads/2008/01/a-new-generation-a-new-commitment-to-change-jan-28-2008.pdf.

4   Tiffani Lennon, *Benchmarking Women's Leadership in the United States* (Denver: University of Denver, Colorado Women's College, 2013), https://www.issuelab.org/resources/26706/26706.pdf.

5   "Women in Management: Quick Take," Catalyst, Research, August 11, 2020, https://www.catalyst.org/research/women-in -management/.

6   Judith Warner, Nora Ellman, and Diane Boesch, "The Women's Leadership Gap," Center for American Progress, November 20, 2018, https://www.americanprogress.org/issues/women/ reports/2018/11/20/461273/womens-leadership-gap-2/.

7   Kristen Joiner, "Like the Vacuuming, Nonprofit Work Is Women's Work," *Stanford Social Innovation Review*, June 12, 2015, https://ssir .org/articles/entry/like_the_vacuuming_nonprofit_work_is_womens_ work.

8   *Merriam-Webster*, s.v., "charity (*n.*)," accessed August 28, 2020, https://www.merriam-webster.com/dictionary/charity.

9   Melissa de Witte, "Stanford Scholar Addresses the Problems with Philanthropy," Stanford, News, December 2, 2018, https://news .stanford.edu/2018/12/03/the-problems-with-philanthropy/.

10 Jane Addams, "The Subtle Problems of Charity," *The Atlantic*, February 1899, https://www.theatlantic.com/magazine/archive/1899/02/ the-subtle-problems-of-charity/306217/.

11 Lester M. Salamon and Chelsea L. Newhouse, *The 2019 Nonprofit Employment Report* (Baltimore: Johns Hopkins Center for Civil Society Studies, 2019), http://ccss.jhu.edu/wp-content/uploads/ downloads/2019/01/2019-NP-Employment-Report_FINAL_1.8 .2019.pdf. Based on 2016 data from U.S. Bureau of Labor Statistics.

12 *Nonprofit Impact Matters: How America's Charitable Nonprofits Strengthen Communities and Improve Lives* (Washington, D.C.: National Council of Nonprofits, 2019).

13   Adapted from "Chapter 3: Philanthropy and Public Policy," Our
     State of Generosity, accessed August 28, 2020, https://ourstateof
     generosity.org/section/role-of-philanthropy-four-sector-society/.

14   Forbes Nonprofit Council, "12 Effective Ways to Operate a Nonprofit
     Like a For-Profit Business," *Forbes*, March 7, 2018, https://www
     .forbes.com/sites/forbesnonprofitcouncil/2018/03/07/12-effective
     -ways-to-operate-a-nonprofit-like-a-for-profit-business/#77b97c6
     034c6.

15   Soren Kaplan, "The Future of Nonprofits: Run Them Like an
     Innovative Business," *Inc.*, January 8, 2018, https://www.inc.com/
     soren-kaplan/the-future-of-non-profits-run-it-like-an-innovative
     -business.html.

16   Sarah L. Pettijohn and Elizabeth T. Boris, *Nonprofit-Government
     Contracts and Grants: Findings from the 2013 National Survey* (Wash-
     ington, D.C.: Urban Institute, 2013), https://www.urban.org/sites/
     default/files/publication/24231/412962-Nonprofit-Government
     -Contracts-and-Grants-Findings-from-the-National-Survey.pdf.

17   "Facts: Wealth Inequality in the United States," Inequality.org,
     accessed August 28, 2020, https://inequality.org/facts/wealth
     -inequality/. See also Steve Dubb, "The Economy Is Changing—
     and So Must We: A New Charge for Nonprofits," *NPO Nonprofit
     Quarterly*, July 9, 2018, https://nonprofitquarterly.org/the-economy
     -is-changing-and-so-must-we-a-new-charge-for-nonprofits/.

18   Chuck Collins, Josh Hoxie, and Helen Flannery, *Gilded Giving 2018:
     Top-Heavy Philanthropy and Its Perils to the Independent Sector and
     Democracy* (Washington, D.C.: Institute for Policy Studies, 2018), 5,
     https://inequality.org/wp-content/uploads/2018/11/Gilded-Giving
     -November-2018-FINAL.pdf.

19   Stephen Fishman, "How Much Lobbying Can a Nonprofit Do?"
     Nolo, accessed August 28, 2020, https://www.nolo.com/legal
     -encyclopedia/how-much-lobbying-can-nonprofit-do.html.

20   *Nonprofit Impact Matters*, 34.

21 Tim Delaney, "Advocating for the Value Nonprofits Create: An Interview with Tim Delaney," interviewed by Nell Edgington, Social Velocity, October 27, 2015, https://www.socialvelocity.net/2015/10/27/advocating-for-the-value-nonprofits-create-an-interview -with-tim-delaney/.

22 Jeri Eckhart-Queenan, Michael Etzel, and Sridhar Prasad, "Pay-What-It-Takes Philanthropy," The Bridgespan Group, May 15, 2016, https://www.bridgespan.org/insights/library/pay-what-it-takes/pay-what-it-takes-philanthropy.

23 Art Taylor, Jacob Harold, and Ken Berger, "Letter to the Donors of America," The Overhead Myth, accessed August 28, 2020, http://overheadmyth.com/letter-to-the-donors-of-america/.

24 Rick Moyers, "There's No Penalty for Having Reserves," *The Chronicle of Philanthropy*, May 6, 2011, https://www.philanthropy.com/article/Theres-No-Penalty-for-Having/190573.

25 "State of the Nonprofit Sector Survey 2018 Key Findings," Survey Analyzer, accessed August 28, 2020, https://nff.org/surveydata.

26 Pippa Stevens, "Here Are the 10 Companies with the Most Cash On Hand," CNBC, November 7, 2019, https://www.cnbc.com/2019/11/07/microsoft-apple-and-alphabet-are-sitting-on-more-than-100 -billion-in-cash.html.

27 Will Yakowicz, "The Biggest Philanthropic Gifts of 2019," *Forbes*, December 29, 2019, https://www.forbes.com/sites/willyakowicz/2020/12/29/the-top-10-philanthropic-gifts-of-2019/#65b630 b67946.

28 Jason D. Rowley, "The Most Recent Startup Investments Over $250 Million in 2019," *Crunchbase News*, June 17, 2019, https://news.crunchbase.com/news/the-most-recent-startup-investments -over-250-million-in-2019/.

29 Tara Mohr, *Playing Big: Practical Wisdom for Women Who Want to Speak Up, Create, and Lead* (New York: Avery, 2015), 249.

Chapter Two

Epigraph: America Ferrera in *Shine On with Reese*, episode 7, executive producer Reese Witherspoon, aired 2019, Netflix, https://www
.netflix.com/title/81169914.

1   John R.P. French Jr. and Bertram Raven, "The Bases of Social Power,"
in *Studies in Social Power*, ed. D. Cartwright (Ann Arbor: University
of Michigan, 1959), 150–67, http://www.communicationcache.com/
uploads/1/0/8/8/10887248/the_bases_of_social_power_-_chapter_
20_-_1959.pdf.

2   Brené Brown, *Braving the Wilderness: The Quest for True Belonging and
the Courage to Stand Alone* (New York: Random House, 2017), 156.

3   Karen Kleiman, "Are You an Over-Giver?" *Psychology Today*, March
26, 2014, https://www.psychologytoday.com/us/blog/isnt-what-i
-expected/201403/are-you-over-giver-1.

4   Adapted from psychologist Abraham Maslow's original hierarchy
of human needs. See Saul McLeod, "Maslow's Hierarchy of Needs,"
Simply Psychology, updated March 20, 2020, https://www.simply
psychology.org/maslow.html.

5   It's a cool story. See "Raising Men Lawn Care Service: Giving Back
to the Community," R.M.L.C.S., accessed September 6, 2020,
https://weareraisingmen.com/.

6   Adapted from Gay Hendricks, *The Big Leap: Conquer Your Hidden
Fear and Take Life to the Next Level* (New York: HarperOne, 2010).

Chapter Three

Epigraph: Jay Parini, "A Place Apart: The Spirit of Frost Lives On in
His Cabin," *Middlebury College Magazine* 75, no. 4 (2001): 36.

1   Ann Goggins Gregory and Don Howard, "The Nonprofit Starvation
Cycle," *Stanford Social Innovation Review*, Fall 2009, https://ssir.org/
articles/entry/the_nonprofit_starvation_cycle.

2   Tim Delaney, "Guest Post: The Rebirth of Nonprofit Advocacy," March 5, 2017, https://www.socialvelocity.net/2017/03/05/the -rebirth-of-nonprofit-advocacy/.

3   Alex Tribou and Keith Collins, "This is How Fast America Changes Its Mind," *Bloomberg Business*, updated June 26, 2015, http://www .bloomberg.com/graphics/2015-pace-of-social-change/.

4   Alison Beard, "Making a Backup Plan Undermines Performance," *Harvard Business Review*, September 2016, https://hbr.org/2016/09/ making-a-backup-plan-undermines-performance.

5   "A Commitment to Philanthropy," The Giving Pledge, accessed August 28, 2020, https://givingpledge.org/.

6   Alana Semuels, "Paul Allen Shows It's Hard to Give Away $10 Billion," *The Atlantic*, October 16, 2018, https://www.theatlantic .com/technology/archive/2018/10/paul-allen-shows-its-hard-to -donate-10-billion/573109/.

7   William Foster, Gail Perreault, Alison Powell, and Chris Addy, "Making Big Bets for Social Change," *Stanford Social Innovation Review*, Winter 2016, https://ssir.org/articles/entry/making_big_ bets_for_social_change.

8   "Sesame Street: Janelle Monáe—Power of Yet," from *Sesame Street*, episode 4502, "Bert's Training Wheels," aired September 16, 2014, video, 2:41, September 10, 2014, https://www.youtube.com/ watch?v=XLeUvZvuvAs.

9   "Robert Emmons," *Greater Good Magazine*, Profile, accessed August 28, 2020, https://greatergood.berkeley.edu/profile/ Robert_Emmons.

Chapter Four

Epigraph: Julia Cameron, "God Is Extravagant," The Artist's Way, February 8, 2012, https://juliacameronlive.com/2012/02/08/ god-is-extravagant.

1   *Nonprofit Impact Matters: How America's Charitable Nonprofits
    Strengthen Communities and Improve Lives* (Washington, D.C.:
    National Council of Nonprofits, 2019), https://www.nonprofit
    impactmatters.org/site/assets/files/1/nonprofit-impact-matters
    -sept-2019-1.pdf. Based on data from IRS Business Master Files,
    Revenue Transaction Files, and electronic (e-File) Form 990 returns
    processed for fiscal years ending circa 2016 (June 2018) by Data-
    Lake Nonprofit Research (datalake.net), Urban Institute's National
    Center for Charitable Statistics.

2   Marcia Garcia Abadia and Johnny Lin, "Nonprofit Cost Analysis
    Toolkit," The Bridgespan Group, June 3, 2009, https://www
    .bridgespan.org/insights/library/pay-what-it-takes/nonprofit-cost
    -analysis-introduction.

3   In *Good to Great for the Social Sector: Why Business Thinking Is Not the
    Answer* (New York: HarperCollins, 2005), 19, Jim Collins calls this
    the "Hedgehog Concept"; in *Creating Public Value: Strategic Man-
    agement in Government* (Cambridge, MA: Harvard University Press,
    1995), Mark Moore calls it "The Strategic Triangle."

4   The Leap Ambassadors community, of which I am a member,
    has developed The Performance Practice, an in-depth organi-
    zational self-assessment tool. See "The Performance Practice,"
    Leap of Reason Ambassadors Community, accessed August 28,
    2020, https://leapambassadors.org/continuous-improvement/
    performance-practice/.

5   Cynthia M. Gibson, *Beyond Fundraising: What Does It Mean to Build
    a Culture of Philanthropy?* (San Francisco: Evelyn and Walter Haas
    Jr. Fund, 2016), 9, https://www.haasjr.org/sites/default/files/
    resources/Haas_CultureofPhilanthropy_F1_0.pdf.

6   Jeanne Bell and Maria Cornelius, *UnderDeveloped: A National Study
    of Challenges Facing Nonprofit Fundraising* (Oakland: CompassPoint,
    2013), https://www.compasspoint.org/underdeveloped.

7   For example, Edgar Villanueva, *Decolonizing Wealth: Indigenous Wisdom to Heal Divides and Restore Balance* (Oakland: Berrett-Koehler Publishers, 2018); and Anand Giridharadas, *Winners Take All: The Elite Charade of Changing the World* (New York: Vintage, 2019).

Chapter Five

Epigraph: Willa Cather, *My Ántonia* (Boston: Houghton Mifflin, 1988), 14.

1   Kerry Patterson, Joseph Grenny, Ron McMillan, and Al Switzler, *Crucial Conversations: Tools for Talking When Stakes Are High*, 2nd ed. (New York: McGraw Hill, 2012).

2   Jane Wei-Skillern and Sonia Marciano, "The Networked Nonprofit," *Stanford Social Innovation Review*, Spring 2008, https://ssir.org/articles/entry/the_networked_nonprofit.

3   Jane Wei-Skillern, David Ehrlichman, and David Sawyer, "The Most Impactful Leaders You Have Never Heard Of," *Stanford Social Innovation Review*, September 16, 2015, https://ssir.org/articles/entry/the_most_impactful_leaders_youve_never_heard_of#.

4   NPR Staff, "'Don't Know'? Just Admit It," NPR, September 18, 2013, https://www.npr.org/2013/09/18/223402246/dont-know-just-admit-it.

5   Wikipedia, s.v., "*shoshin*," accessed August 28, 2020, https://en.wikipedia.org/wiki/Shoshin.

6   Dallon Adams, "The Best of Biomimicry: Here's 7 Brilliant Examples of Nature-Inspired Design," *Digital Trends*, January 28, 2017, https://www.digitaltrends.com/cool-tech/biomimicry-examples/.

7   Tim Delaney, "Advocating for the Value Nonprofits Create: An Interview with Tim Delaney," interviewed by Nell Edgington, Social Velocity, October 27, 2015, https://www.socialvelocity.net/2015/10/27/advocating-for-the-value-nonprofits-create-an-interview-with-tim-delaney/.

8   "Rules of Advocacy & Lobbying," Council on Foundations, accessed August 28, 2020, https://www.cof.org/content/rules-advocacy -lobbying.

9   "Tools & Resources," National Council of Nonprofits, accessed August 28, 2020, https://www.councilofnonprofits.org/tools -resources-categories/advocacy; "Stand for Your Mission," Stand for Your Mission, accessed August 28, 2020, https://standforyour mission.org/.

10 "Rules of Advocacy & Lobbying," Council on Foundations.

Conclusion

Epigraph: June Jordan, "Poem for South African Women," from *Passion* (1980), http://www.junejordan.net/poem-for-south-african -women.html.

1   Nancy Koehn, "Closing Keynote Speech" (lecture, Center for Effective Philanthropy conference, Boston, MA, April 2017). See also, Nell Edgington, "Can Philanthropy Lead in Challenging Times," Social Velocity, April 11, 2017, https://www.socialvelocity.net/2017/04/11/ can-philanthropy-lead-in-these-challenging-times/.

Acknowledgments

Epigraph: See Ram Dass and Mirabai Bush, "Walking Each Other Home: Conversations on Loving and Dying," Ram Dass, accessed September 6, 2020, https://www.ramdass.org/walking-each -other-home/.

Further Reading

Epigraph: William Nicholson, *Shadowlands: A Play* (New York: Plume, 1991).

"We read to know
we're not alone."

WILLIAM NICHOLSON

Further Reading

N MY JOURNEY over the past several years to *Reinventing Social Change*, countless writers, in addition to the sources listed in the notes section, helped point the way. Below are some that you, too, might find useful.

Baldwin, James. *The Fire Next Time*. New York: Vintage, 1993. First published 1963 by The Dial Press (New York).

Beck, Martha. *Finding Your Way in a Wild New World: Reclaim Your True Nature to Create the Life You Want*. New York: Atria, 2013.

brown, adrienne maree. *Emergent Strategy: Shaping Change, Changing Worlds*. Chico, CA: AK Press, 2017.

Cain, Susan. *Quiet: The Power of Introverts in a World That Can't Stop Talking*. New York: Crown, 2012.

Cameron, Julia. *The Vein of Gold: A Journey to Your Creative Heart*. New York: Jeremy P. Tarcher/Putnam, 1997.

Dweck, Carol. *Mindset: The New Psychology of Success*. New York: Ballantine Books, 2016. First published 2006 by Random House (New York).

Gilbert, Elizabeth. *Big Magic: Creative Living Beyond Fear*. New York: Riverhead Books, 2015.

Grout, Pam. *Art & Soul, Reloaded: A Yearlong Apprenticeship for Summoning the Muses and Reclaiming Your Bold, Audacious, Creative Side*. Carlsbad: Hay House, 2017.

Jackson, Laura Lynn. *Signs: The Secret Language of the Universe*. New York: The Dial Press, 2020.

Lynch, David. *Catching the Big Fish: Meditation, Consciousness, and Creativity*. New York: Penguin Group, 2006.

Morrow Lindbergh, Anne. *Gift from the Sea*. New York: Vintage Books (Random House), 1991.

Nhất Hạnh, Thích. *The Art of Living*. New York: HarperCollins, 2017.

Silver, Tosha. *Outrageous Openness: Letting the Divine Take the Lead*. New York: Atria Books, 2014.

Sincero, Jen. *You Are a Badass at Making Money: Master the Mindset of Wealth*. New York: Viking, 2017.

Tolle, Eckhart. *The Power of Now: A Guide to Spiritual Enlightenment*. Novato, CA: New World Library, 2004.

Wright, Robert. *Why Buddhism is True: The Science and Philosophy of Meditation and Enlightenment*. New York: Simon and Schuster, 2017.

About the Author

NELL EDGINGTON has spent her twenty-five-year career innovating in the social change sector. As president of Social Velocity, she helps create more strategic, financially savvy, and confident nonprofit and philanthropic leaders and organizations. Nell is a popular writer, speaker, and blogger, and co-author of *The Strategic Management of Charter Schools: Frameworks and Tools for Educational Entrepreneurs*. She is a member of the national Leap Ambassadors Community, a network of more than 250 social change thought leaders. Nell holds an MBA from the Kellogg School of Management at Northwestern University.

www.socialvelocity.net
www.twitter.com/nedgington
www.linkedin.com/in/nelledgington